P9-CKE-778

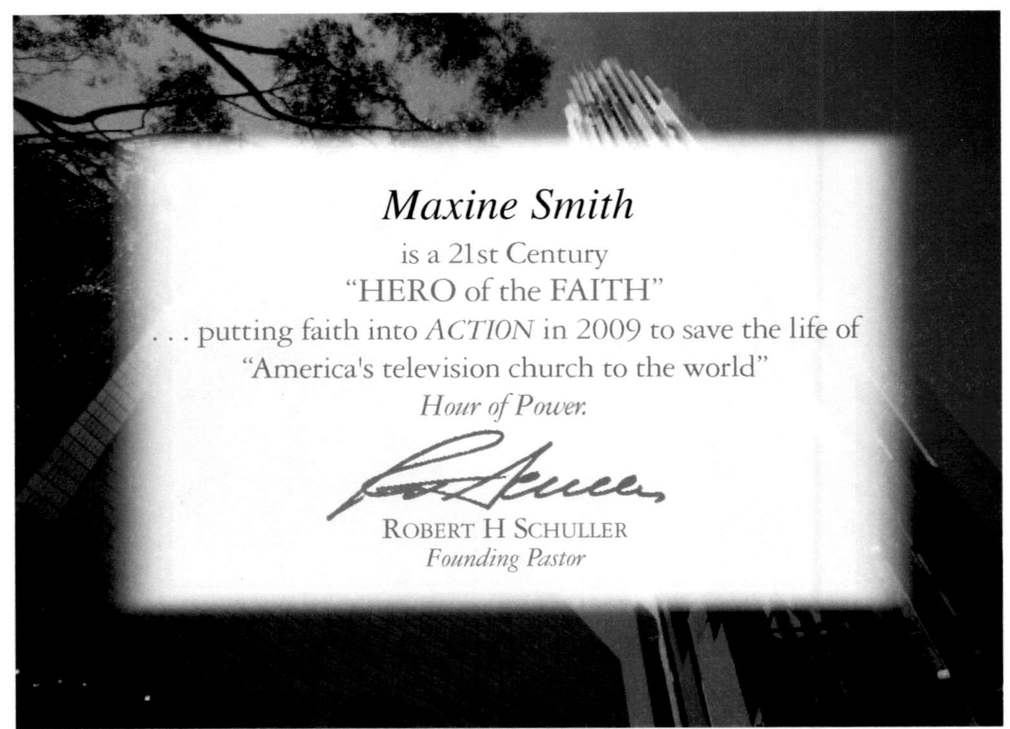
Maxine Smith
is a 21st Century
"HERO of the FAITH"
. . . putting faith into ACTION in 2009 to save the life of
"America's television church to the world"
Hour of Power.
ROBERT H SCHULLER
Founding Pastor

HOUR OF POWER

Acts of the Apostles

Jesus said …"Most assuredly, I say to you, unless one is born again, he cannot see the kingdom of God … unless one is born of water and the Spirit, he cannot enter the kingdom of God."

JOHN 3:3, 5

THOMAS NELSON
Since 1798

NASHVILLE DALLAS MEXICO CITY RIO DE JANEIRO BEIJING

PANOGRAPHS BY KEN DUNCAN

HOUR OF POWER Acts of the Apostles

ACTS OF THE APOSTLES
HOUR OF POWER

PUBLISHED BY THOMAS NELSON, INC.
501 NELSON PLACE, NASHVILLE, TN, 37214, USA

PHOTOGRAPHY AND TEXT: KEN DUNCAN,
COPYRIGHT © 2009 DIVINE GUIDANCE PTY. LIMITED
DESIGN: PETER MORLEY, GOOD CATCH DESIGN
MAP ILLUSTRATIONS: JOHN BULL, THE BOOK DESIGN CO.
CO-AUTHOR: IRENE VOYSEY
EDITOR: OWEN SALTER, BARNABAS EDITORIAL SERVICES AND TRAINING
REPROGRAPHICS: CFL PRINT STUDIO, AUSTRALIA.
www.createdforlife.com
PRODUCTION: PANOGRAPHS PUBLISHING PTY. LIMITED, PART OF THE KEN DUNCAN GROUP
PRINTED AND BOUND IN CHINA
ISBN 9781-40411-403-6

FOR MORE INFORMATION ABOUT KEN DUNCAN AND HIS WORK VISIT **www.kenduncan.com**

Front Cover
FIRST CENTURY A.D. REPLICA BOAT CALLED KERYNEIA LIBERTY, CYPRUS.

Title Page
CLAY AMPHORAS USED FOR CARRYING SUPPLIES SIMILAR TO THOSE THAT WOULD HAVE BEEN CARRIED BY PAUL ON HIS JOURNEY; CYPRUS. FROM REPLICA BOAT CALLED KERYNEIA LIBERTY.

Endpapers
PAINTING FROM THE CHURCH OF ST LAZARUS, PALESTINE

SELEUCIA BEACH, TURKEY
Paul would have visited this beach on his first missionary journey.

Jesus … spoke to them saying, "All authority has been given to Me in heaven and on earth. Go therefore and make disciples of all the nations, baptizing them in the name of the Father and of the Son and of the Holy Spirit." MATTHEW 28:18-19

SUNSET OVER JERUSALEM

THE HOLY SPIRIT IS PROMISED

Foreword

And being assembled together with them, He [Jesus] commanded them not to depart from Jerusalem, but to wait for the Promise of the Father, "which," He said, "you have heard from Me; for John truly baptized with water, but you shall be baptized with the Holy Spirit not many days from now." Therefore, when they had come together, they asked Him, saying, "Lord, will You at this time restore the kingdom to Israel?" And He said to them, "It is not for you to know times or seasons which the Father has put in His own authority. But you shall receive power when the Holy Spirit has come upon you; and you shall be witnesses to Me in Jerusalem, and in all Judea and Samaria, and to the end of the earth."

ACTS 1:4-8

Following Jesus is a call to action—action that is securely rooted in possibility-thinking faith and fully empowered by the Holy Spirit. It's the kind of faith-in-action Matthew described when he wrote, "If you have faith as small as a mustard seed, you can say to this mountain, 'Move from here to there' and it will move. Nothing will be impossible for you" (Matthew 17:20 NIV).

It's the kind of faith I experienced in 1955 as a twenty-eight-year-old preacher who said "yes" to building a church in a developing suburb in Southern California. I had no buildings and no land, but I did have $500 and a God-given dream to do something great for Him. My dream was met with a mixture of skepticism and amusement when I asked the manager of the Orange Drive-in Theater if I could hold services there. He agreed. With God as my encourager, I enthusiastically went to work building a large cross for the top of the snack bar so people in their cars would know it was, indeed, a church.

Many of my peers scoffed at my idea of a drive-in church, and from time to time doubts crept into my mind. Yet down deep in my heart I knew I was following God's plan for a dynamic church that would present the positive, life-changing message of Jesus Christ needed by the people in the community where God had led us. My faith had resolve and I held on to the belief that the vision God had placed in my heart to make Christ known would come to be. And it did!

Twenty centuries earlier and thousands of miles from Southern California, God was working through a small group of ordinary followers of Jesus to accomplish his work in the world as they opened themselves to the Spirit's call and found new direction and new purpose for their lives. Their story was recorded in the New Testament's Book of Acts. And now, through the help of our great friend and very talented partner in ministry, Ken Duncan, you can retrace the acts of the apostles as their story unfolds in this exquisitely photographed book.

Ken visited many nations on numerous occasions to retrace the footsteps of the early apostles and capture their story photographically. Through the lens of his camera you will catch a glimpse of the power and impact of the Holy Spirit at Pentecost. You will witness the transforming power of change in the life of the apostle Peter. You'll travel down the road to Gaza with Philip, a man "full of the Spirit and wisdom," where he explains to an Ethiopian government official the good news of Jesus Christ. And you'll accompany the apostle Paul on all three of his missionary journeys, each one captured as accurately as humanly possible with a camera.

I've been to many of the places Ken has included in *Acts of the Apostles* and know the powerful impact seeing them can have in one's life. We are called to make a positive difference in the world. My prayer is that the photographs and narratives in this book will first transport you and then transform you as the Holy Spirit empowers you to follow the vision God has placed in your heart.

ROBERT H. SCHULLER, FOUNDING PASTOR
CRYSTAL CATHEDRAL, HOUR OF POWER

PARTHENON FROM PHILOPAPPOU HILL, ATHENS, GREECE

In a city with many false gods, the apostle Paul proclaimed Jesus, who said, "I am the way, the truth, and the life. No one comes to the Father except through Me".

Jesus said, "You are the light of the world. A city that is set on a hill cannot be hidden …
Let your light so shine before men, that they may see your good works and glorify your Father in heaven.' MATTHEW 5:14,16

DEDICATION

This book is dedicated to the Holy Spirit, in whom we have enabling power to follow the vision God has placed in our hearts to make Christ known.

KEN DUNCAN

ICON, ABBEY OF SAINT PAUL'S VISION, KAUKAB, SYRIA

This icon shows Paul falling from his horse on the road to Damascus.

A PROPHECY OF JOEL

"And it shall come to pass afterward
That I will pour out My Spirit on all flesh;
Your sons and your daughters shall prophesy,
Your old men shall dream dreams,
Your young men shall see visions.
And also on My menservants and on My maidservants
I will pour out My Spirit in those days..."

JOEL 2:28–29

BLUE LAGOON, GOZO, MALTA
Paul was shipwrecked in Malta. While waiting for a new boat he spread the good news about Jesus.

ACTS OF THE APOSTLES

Contents

THE UPPER ROOM, JERUSALEM, ISRAEL

This is believed to be the location of the place where the disciple received the power of the Holy Spirit, just as Jesus had promised.

Introduction

When the Day of Pentecost had fully come, they were all with one accord in one place.
And suddenly there came a sound from heaven, as of a rushing mighty wind, and it filled the whole house where they were sitting.
Then there appeared to them divided tongues, as of fire, and one sat upon each of them.
And they were all filled with the Holy Spirit and began to speak with other tongues, as the Spirit gave them utterance.

ACTS 2:1-4

I am so thankful for Dr Robert H. Schuller and his ministry, and I am honored to be producing this book for the Crystal Cathedral. I hope it will bless others as they have blessed me, and generate more finances for the ministry to continue its great work. Many years ago, Dr Schuller's message of faith reached me across continents through his television program, *Hour of Power*. At the time I felt broken and hopeless, but his message inspired me to reach up and grab the hand of Jesus. I thank God for Dr Schuller—to me he is a modern-day apostle.

Some years ago I was privileged to be invited to shoot on the set of the famous Mel Gibson movie *The Passion of the Christ*, where I focused on Christ's last days. Being on the set was like being transported back in time to the actual days of Jesus. It reminded me of the supreme price Jesus paid for my salvation.

I was so challenged by that experience I decided to explore the places Jesus actually lived and traveled. Connecting with the locations of Jesus' life helped me get an even greater understanding of His reality. That expedition culminated in another book called *Where Jesus Walked*, and after that I wondered how anyone could not believe in Jesus if they honestly looked at the overwhelming body of evidence of His life.

The experience of photographing those two books was challenging, but in both cases it was all about what Jesus had done. His walk, His death, and His resurrection can change our lives forever if we believe. The next adventure was to be quite different—it would challenge me as to what I was going to do with the example of Jesus' walk when I truly understood its reality and cost.

I was drawn to follow the journeys of some of the early believers. Paul and Peter were two I could really relate to. Prior to Christ I had been vicious towards Christianity, like Paul (Saul), and a bit of a rough diamond, like Peter. Paul had been on the road to Damascus—on his way to kill the followers of Jesus—and had to be struck off his high horse before he saw the light of Christ.

I admit I didn't really want to follow in the footsteps of the early apostles as I knew it would really challenge me in my own walk with God. Paul was a man just like me, born with the seed of sin and prone to all the same temptations. Yet looking closely at his life made me realize how far I still had to go as a believer. Paul was totally sold out for Jesus—he devoted his life to spreading the Gospel message. Peter was a fisherman who made many mistakes, even denying Christ three times. I have spent time with modern-day fishermen at the Sea of Galilee and nothing much has changed. It's a tough life. It just goes to show how Jesus can transform lives if we will allow Him. On the day of Pentecost, when the Holy Spirit came upon Peter, he shared so effectively about Jesus that 3000 people came to know Christ. This was no speech by a mere fisherman. This was a man who believed in Jesus and allowed the Holy Spirit to move through him.

Paul and Peter were people who showed the importance of moving in the power of the Holy Spirit, and I believe these patriarchs of Christianity have a crucial message for us even today. We need the power of the Holy Spirit in our lives, and the sign of that power is a life that is transformed and on fire for Jesus. I hope the photos and inspirational text in this book help to convey the commitment of the early believers, and that their example may encourage you as much as it has me to live a life that glorifies Jesus.

Capturing the photographs for this book was really one of the most challenging projects I've ever undertaken. I'm not saying that all the apostles' journeys were precisely as depicted, but I have attempted to be as accurate as possible.

Blessings for the road ahead.

Ken Duncan.

ACKNOWLEDGEMENTS

Firstly, I would like to thank my beautiful wife, Pamela, and my wonderful daughter, Jessica, for their love and support while I was on this journey. Thank you also to my good friend Charlie Asmar, the greatest guide in Israel, Palestine and Jordan (charlieasmar@yahoo.com).

Thanks also to my other great guides:

- *Azim Tours Travel in Turkey (azimtours@superonline.com)*
- *Photos Hadjihambi in Cyprus (photos@kyprotours.com.cy)*
- *Angela at Malta Tourism Authority (www.visitmalta.com)*

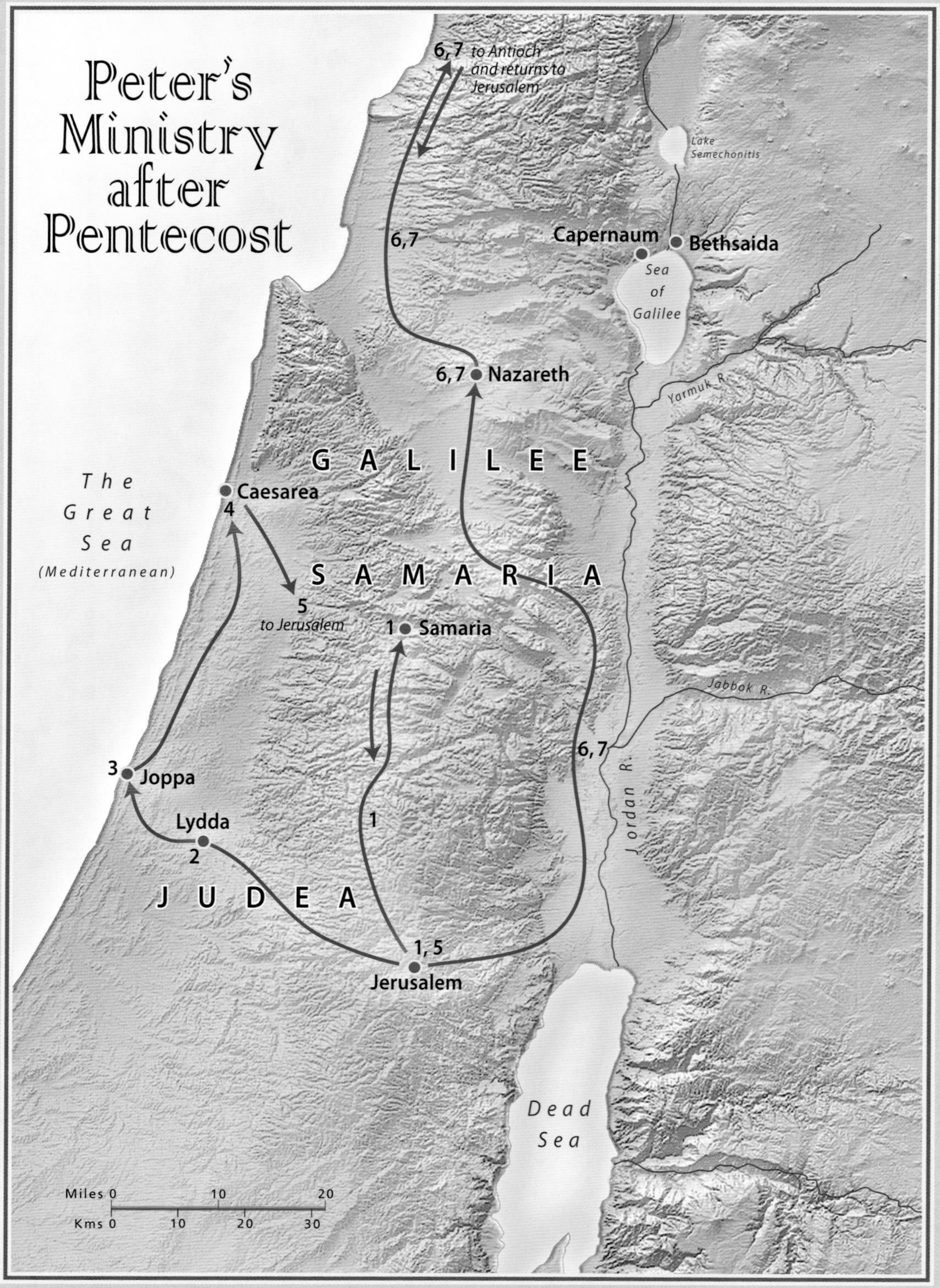

KEY

1. The first return missionary trip from Jerusalem to Samaria by Peter and John. Acts 8:14–17

2. On his second trip Peter heals Aeneas of palsy at Lydda. Acts 9:32–36

3. In Joppa Peter raises Tabitha from the dead Acts 9:36–43 and sees a vision from heaven. Acts 10:9–16

4. Peter meets the Roman centurion at Caesarea. Acts 10:23–48

5. Peter returns to Jerusalem and is delivered from prison by an angel. Acts 12:3–10

6. Peter goes on his third journey to Antioch and returns to Jerusalem. Acts 15:1–14; Galatians 2:11

7. Peter leaves Jerusalem traveling through the empire to Rome where he is martyred. Tradition and other sources

Lines show only general direction and approximate sequence of journeys.

→ Peter's Journey

● Generally accepted or known location

MOSAIC IN BASILICA OF SAINT PAUL OUTSIDE THE WALLS, ROME, ITALY

Therefore being exalted to the right hand of God, and having received from the Father the promise of the Holy Spirit, He [Jesus] poured out this which you now see and hear.

ACTS 2:33

ACTS OF THE APOSTLES

Peter after Pentecost

The time had finally come! This was the time when God would pour out His Spirit on all people; the time promised by the Lord six centuries earlier through the prophet Joel.

The coming of the Spirit in that phenomenal hour did not end with the followers of Jesus who were gathered in a simple room in Jerusalem. The transforming power of the Spirit would soon move beyond the Jewish nation, fulfilling Joel's centuries-old prophecy that God would pour out His Spirit on all people.

Peter the coward, who had denied that he was a follower of Jesus just weeks before, became Peter, the courageous first leader of the Christian church. He knew the words of Joel's prophecy well, so he also knew God's warning that the Day of Judgment was coming. The people of Joel's day were told that the only way they could escape God's anger on all sinful people was to repent.

Peter had repented of all his sins and had mourned his denial of Jesus; he had turned to God with all his heart. Then, while he obediently waited and prayed in Jerusalem, just as Jesus had told the disciples to do, he was transformed forever by God's Spirit.

We are privileged to live in "those days" that God referred to in Joel's warning; a warning repeated by Peter. These are the days between the ascension of Jesus and His return—the last days.

The Spirit of God enabled Peter and other uneducated Galileans to proclaim the risen Christ with courage, confidence and conviction. This transforming power of the Spirit is the same power that can be poured out into your life today.

The record of the acts of the followers of Jesus is clear and visible evidence of the invisible Holy Spirit empowering ordinary people. Until God's saving message goes out to the ends of the earth, the same Spirit will lovingly, patiently and generously continue to inspire, lead, teach, rebuke, guide, and enable His followers to proclaim the saving love of the Lord Jesus Christ.

Be encouraged—it is God's aim to fill you with His Spirit!

TEMPLE MOUNT, JERUSALEM, ISRAEL.

This is part of Solomon's Porch on the site of Solomon's Temple, an area often used by the first Christians. The gate called Beautiful, referred to in the scripture below, is believed to have been near this location.

... a certain man lame from his mother's womb was ... laid daily at the gate of the temple which is called Beautiful, to ask alms from those who entered the temple; who, seeing Peter and John about to go into the temple, asked for alms. And fixing his eyes on him, with John, Peter said, "Look at us." So he gave them his attention, expecting to receive something from them. Then Peter said, "Silver and gold I do not have, but what I do have I give you: In the name of Jesus Christ of Nazareth, rise up and walk." And he took him by the right hand and lifted him up, and immediately his feet and ankle bones received strength. So he, leaping up, stood and walked and entered the temple with them—walking, leaping, and praising God.

ACTS 3:2-8

Real love produces real miracles. ROBERT H. SCHULLER

ANCIENT MARKETS, LOD (ANCIENT LYDDA), ISRAEL

The prophet Nehemiah, who served as cupbearer to the Persian king Artaxerxes in 444 B.C., placed the city of Lod (also known as Lydda) in the "valley of craftsmen."

When Moses received directions from the Lord about the building of the tabernacle, God gave detailed instructions for the production of gold ornaments by skilled craftsmen. The ornaments included a lamp-stand of pure gold hammered out, its base, shaft, and flower-like cups and blossoms all of one piece. The craftsmen were to be told what sort of flowers they were to shape and where the buds and blossoms were to be. The Lord Himself told Moses he was to invite these and other offerings from the Israelites, "from each man whose heart prompts him to give."

Even as Moses was spending time with the Lord, receiving these instructions, the Israelites were making a calf of gold, which they then bowed down to and worshipped.

The choice of using or abusing material wealth is always before us and examples of both choices are recorded in the Bible.

Jesus' famous saying "Render therefore to Caesar the things that are Caesar's, and to God the things that are God's" was in response to a trick question posed by the Pharisees as they showed him a silver denarius, hoping to trap Him into opposing the Roman taxation laws. The command by Jesus is an all-time reminder to pay our taxes!

For thirty pieces of silver, Judas betrayed his sinless Master.

Peter told the disabled beggar, "Silver and gold I do not have, but what I do have I give you." The healing knowledge of the risen Lord Jesus is beyond value, but it may be given to all, free of charge!

We, who were once spiritually poor but have now received God's Holy Spirit, have also received healing. May we therefore not allow silver and gold to take first place in our lives, but rise up rejoicing, as the beggar did, and gladly go out to share our knowledge with all who want to reach out and receive the saving love of Jesus.

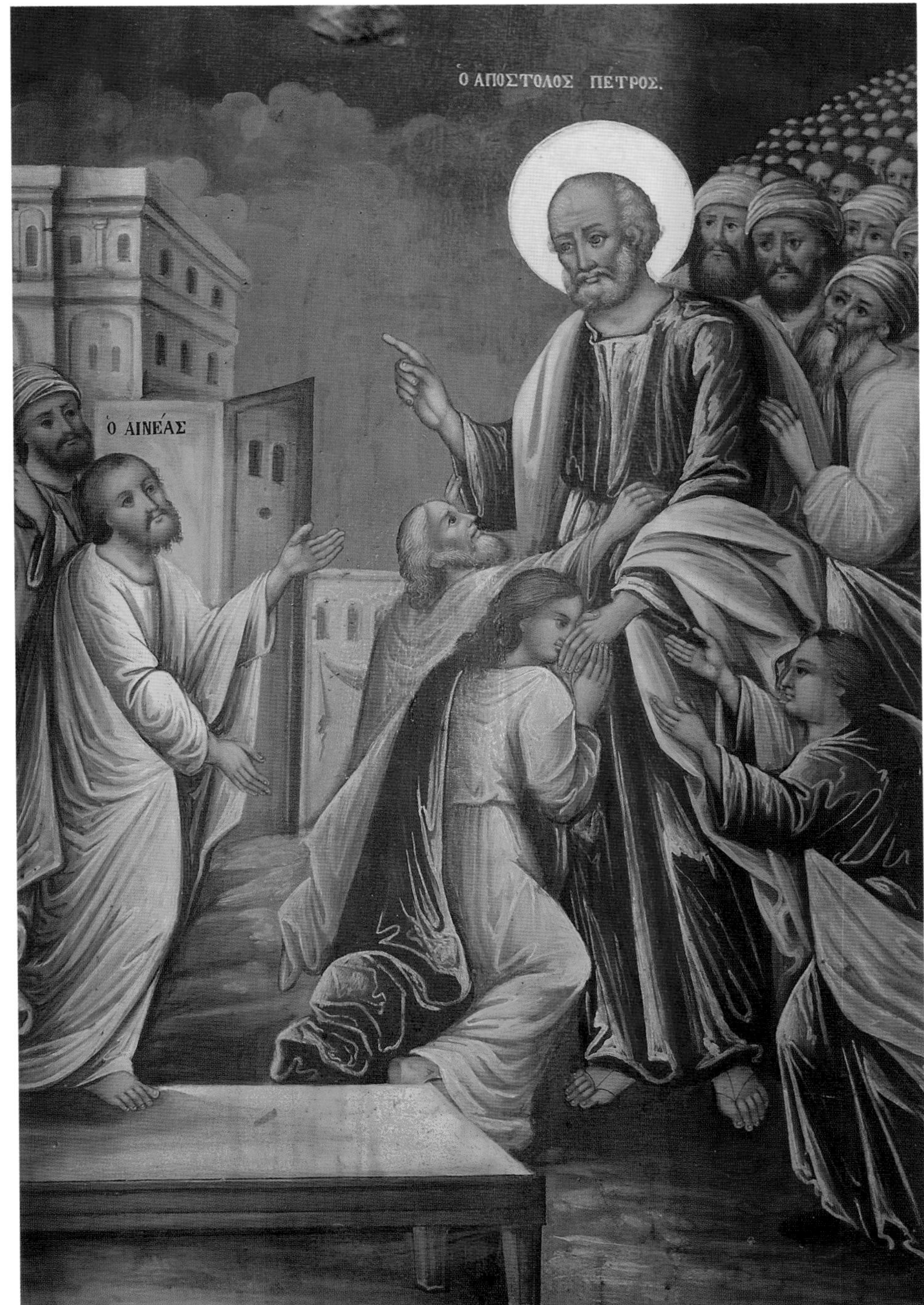

ICON, SAINT GEORGE MONASTRY, LOD (ANCIENT LYDDA), ISRAEL

This is a painting of the healing of Aeneas.

Now it came to pass, as Peter went through all parts of the country, that he also came down to the saints who dwelt in Lydda. There he found a certain man named Aeneas, who had been bedridden eight years and was paralyzed. And Peter said to him, "Aeneas, Jesus the Christ heals you. Arise and make your bed." Then he arose immediately. So all who dwelt at Lydda and Sharon saw him and turned to the Lord.

ACTS 9:32–35

Impossible situations can become possible miracles. ROBERT H. SCHULLER

ROOFTOP OF SIMON THE TANNER'S HOUSE, JAFFA, ISRAEL

This is believed to be the very rooftop on which Peter had his vision from God.

The next step in God's plan of global salvation took place in Jaffa, one of the oldest seaports in the world. Archeological evidence reveals that the port, once called Joppa, has been in use since the Bronze Age. On the rooftop of a house here, the Holy Spirit moved Peter to take that next step. Steeped in Orthodox Jewish tradition, Peter needed to be powerfully moved by God to approach Gentiles (non-Jews). God's move came in an unmistakable way.

It began with a vision, repeated three times, on the rooftop of Simon's house. A sheet was lowered from heaven and opened before Peter. In it were birds and animals that were forbidden food for Jews. Peter was ordered three times to kill and eat. He resisted, but he was commanded by a voice, which he recognized as the voice of God, not to call unclean what God has cleansed.

The vision was immediately followed by Gentile visitors from Caesarea who summoned him to the house of Cornelius, a centurion. During a time of prayer, Cornelius had been told by an angel to send for Peter. When Peter found that Cornelius worshipped the true God, he said, "In truth I perceive that God shows no partiality. But in every nation whoever fears Him and works righteousness is accepted by Him.'

After Peter told Cornelius and his household about the death and resurrection of Jesus for their salvation, the Holy Spirit was poured out on the entire Gentile household. Astonished, Peter and his Jewish friends realized that their message of good news should no longer be restricted to the Jewish nation. The Holy Spirit was undeniably leading the young Christian church to proclaim Christ to Gentile nations as well. (See Acts 10)

JAFFA HARBOR, ISRAEL

At Joppa there was a certain disciple named Tabitha, which is translated Dorcas. This woman was full of good works and charitable deeds which she did. But it happened in those days that she became sick and died. When they had washed her, they laid her in an upper room. And since Lydda was near Joppa, and the disciples had heard that Peter was there, they sent two men to him, imploring him not to delay in coming to them. Then Peter arose and went with them. When he had come, they brought him to the upper room. And all the widows stood by him weeping, showing the tunics and garments which Dorcas had made while she was with them. But Peter put them all out, and knelt down and prayed. And turning to the body he said, "Tabitha, arise." And she opened her eyes, and when she saw Peter she sat up. Then he gave her his hand and lifted her up; and when he had called the saints and widows, he presented her alive. And it became known throughout all Joppa, and many believed on the Lord. So it was that he stayed many days in Joppa with Simon, a tanner. ACTS 9:36-43

Where there's life, there's hope! ROBERT H. SCHULLER

SUNRISE, MAIN BEACH, JAFFA, ISRAEL

Peter said, "In truth I perceive that God shows no partiality. But in every nation whoever fears Him and works righteousness is accepted by Him.' ACTS 10:34-35

There is therefore now no condemnation to those who are in Christ Jesus, who do not walk according to the flesh, but according to the Spirit.

ROMANS 8:1–2

For God so loved the world that He gave His only begotten Son, that whoever believes in Him should not perish but have everlasting life. For God did not send His Son into the world to condemn the world, but that the world through Him might be saved. He who believes in Him is not condemned; but he who does not believe is condemned already, because he has not believed in the name of the only begotten Son of God. And this is the condemnation, that the light has come into the world, and men loved darkness rather than light, because their deeds were evil. For everyone practicing evil hates the light and does not come to the light, lest his deeds should be exposed. But he who does the truth comes to the light, that his deeds may be clearly seen, that they have been done in God."

JOHN 3:16–21

MAIN BEACH, CAESAREA, ISRAEL

God's love blooms when we love each other. ROBERT H. SCHULLER

ALTAR OF SAINT JAMES, BROTHER OF JOHN
It is believed that the body of James is buried beneath this altar in the Church of Saint James, Jerusalem, Israel.

James was the first apostle to be killed. Since then, the persecution of many who follow Christ has continued. Today, thanks to technological advances in communication, we can be informed within hours of the imprisonment, torture, harassment, or death of Christians in other parts of the world.

In our own comfortable corner of the globe, the cost of sharing our faith may come in family division, the derision of workmates, and the loss of friends.

Peter's voice was silenced when he was put behind prison bars for proclaiming Christ; we may find that we have placed ourselves behind bars of our own when we choose to be silent. Personal struggles may rage within us as we recognize our reluctance to open our own mouths and speak of the Savior who died for us. We may justify our silence by telling ourselves that Scripture says only "some are evangelists"; that we are not gifted; that we have other ministries; that we don't know enough Scripture to answer questions if we proclaim Christ on a personal level. And so on.

The solution to these personal struggles is in Scripture. The young Christian church used the most powerful weapon in spiritual warfare: Spirit-led prayer. We are in the very same spiritual war today. Their example is before us, for our learning, in the book of Acts—the acts of the Holy Spirit and therefore the acts of the apostles.

When our mouths are shut, for whatever reason, we need to act. God has poured His love into our hearts by the Holy Spirit, and it is this love, His love for all people, that will move us to actively and wholeheartedly pray for what we dearly want: the doors of our self-imposed prisons to swing open so that we too can go and gladly tell of His love for all people.

SAINT PETER'S PRISON JERUSALEM, ISRAEL

... Herod the king stretched out his hand to harass some from the church. Then he killed James the brother of John with the sword. And because he saw that it pleased the Jews, he proceeded further to seize Peter also. Now it was during the Days of Unleavened Bread. So when he had arrested him, he put him in prison, and delivered him to four squads of soldiers to keep him, intending to bring him before the people after Passover.

Peter was therefore kept in prison, but constant prayer was offered to God for him by the church. And when Herod was about to bring him out, that night Peter was sleeping, bound with two chains between two soldiers; and the guards before the door were keeping the prison. Now behold, an angel of the Lord stood by him, and a light shone in the prison; and he struck Peter on the side and raised him up, saying, "Arise quickly!" And his chains fell off his hands. Then the angel said to him, "Gird yourself and tie on your sandals"; and so he did. And he said to him, "Put on your garment and follow me." So he went out and followed him, and did not know that what was done by the angel was real, but thought he was seeing a vision. When they were past the first and the second guard posts, they came to the iron gate that leads to the city, which opened to them of its own accord; and they went out and went down one street, and immediately the angel departed from him.

ACTS 12:1-10

Where the Spirit of the Lord is, there is liberty. 2 CORINTHIANS 3:17

SAINT PETER'S CHURCH, ANTIOCH, TURKEY

This church is built on the site of the first church building. The word "Christian" was first used here. Antioch became the cradle of Gentile Christianity.

SAINT PETER'S CHAIR AND ALTAR, SAINT PETER'S CHURCH, ANTIOCH, TURKEY

It is believed Peter and Paul sat in this chair.

This building is more than an historical site, and it is more than a reminder of what Peter suffered for the sake of the gospel. It stands as a memorial to true fellowship—an example of how the earliest church members risked their very lives to worship God together and encourage one another in their faith.

The building on this site actually began as a cave in the mountain with many escape tunnels. The stone front was installed later, when it was safer to attend the church.

It was in Antioch that the followers of Jesus were first referred to as Christians. The tenacity of these early believers would have been a powerful witness in this place. Going to church often attracted harsh persecution and sometimes a horrible death, but fear did not stop them from worshiping together. Their commitment is surely an indictment of Christians today who have many lame excuses for staying away from church!

For no other foundation can anyone lay than that which is laid, which is Jesus Christ.

1 CORINTHIANS 3:11

SAINT PETER'S CHURCH, ROME, ITALY

There is considerable scholarly debate about Peter. Little is known about his later years and we are left with fragments of tradition and sources outside the New Testament from which to patch together the full story of his life.

It would seem that Peter left Jerusalem, having been imprisoned for his faith more than once, and continued his ministry elsewhere. He possibly witnessed to Jews who had settled in Babylon and it is believed that this may have been where he wrote his first epistle (1 Peter). It is highly likely that he traveled in the Mediterranean region, continuing to share his eyewitness accounts of the life, death, and resurrection of Jesus.

It is also highly probable that when Mark wrote his Gospel, his accounts were taken directly from Peter's testimony. It is believed that Mark was Peter's translator in Rome, and therefore heard Peter recount the truth about Jesus again and again. Given this repetition of a message, an interpreter like Mark undoubtedly recalled and recorded Peter's eyewitness accounts when he wrote the Gospel of Mark. Peter was therefore the source of the earliest Gospel written about Jesus Christ.

The martyrdom of Peter in Rome is well attested by several ancient writers including Eusebius, Origen, and Irenaeus. Peter probably died in A.D. 64, during the reign of Emperor Nero. According to tradition, he was crucified upside down; it is said that he felt unworthy of dying in the same way as his Lord. He is believed to have been crucified and buried on Vatican Hill. A tomb, thought to be Peter's, was unearthed during excavations under Saint Peter's Basilica, and the high altar of Saint Peter's is the location where Peter's relics have been enshrined.

There are infinite possibilities in little beginnings if God is in them! ROBERT H. SCHULLER

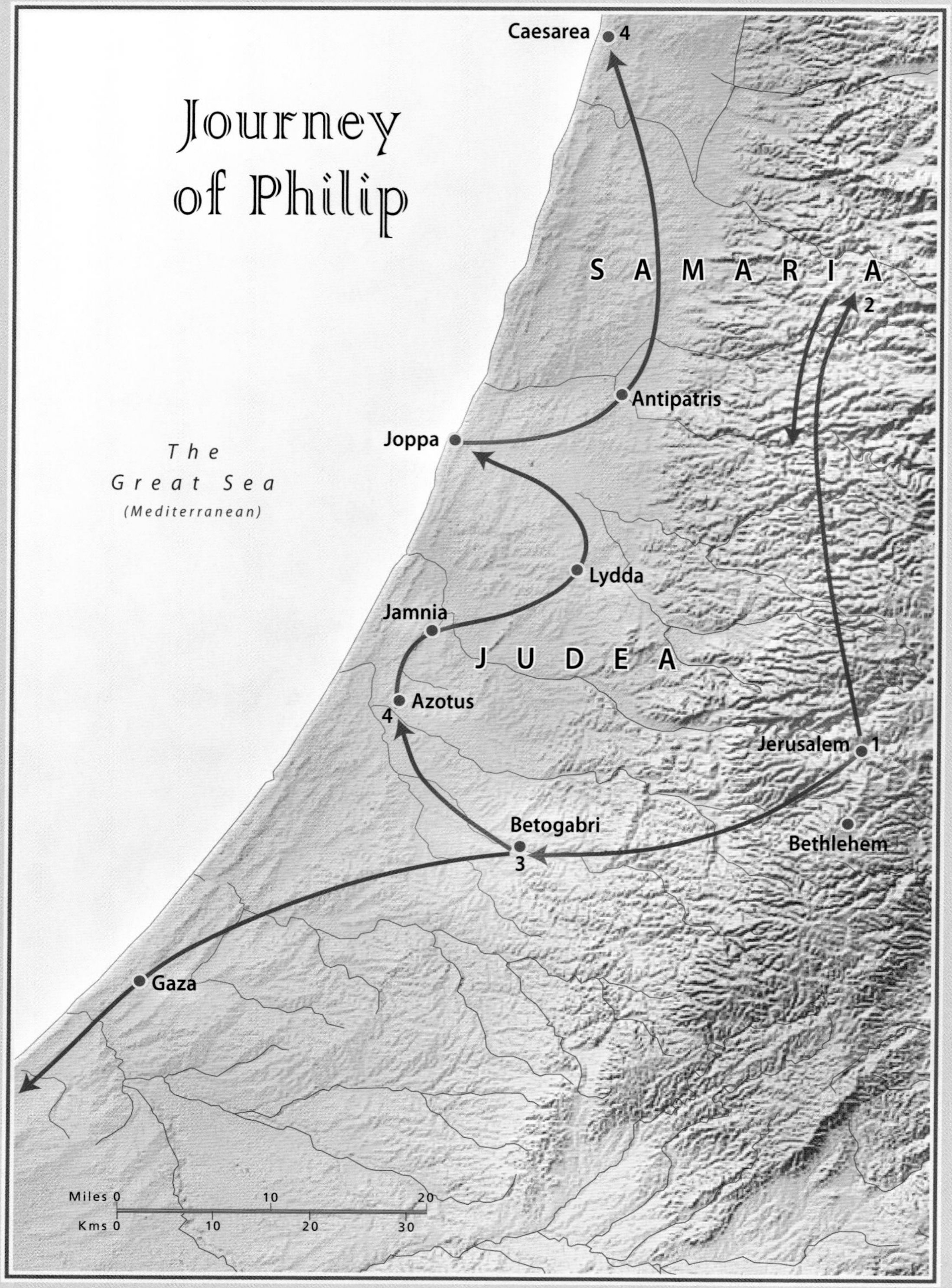

Journey of Philip

Caesarea 4
SAMARIA
2
Antipatris
Joppa
The Great Sea
(Mediterranean)
Lydda
Jamnia
JUDEA
Azotus
4
Jerusalem 1
Betogabri
3
Bethlehem
Gaza
Miles 0 10 20
Kms 0 10 20 30

KEY

1. In Jerusalem Philip is chosen to help the apostles. Acts 6:1–8

2. Philip goes to Samaria. Acts 8:5–25, and returns to Jerusalem where an angel tells him to go to Gaza. Acts 8:26

3. Philip meets an Ethiopian eunuch and baptizes him near Betogabri. Acts 8:37–38

4. Philip is spirited away to Azotus. He preaches along his way to Caesarea. Acts 8:39–40

Lines show only general direction and approximate sequence of journeys.

 Philip's Journey

● Generally accepted or known location

MOSAIC FROM THE BASILICA OF THE TRANSFIGURATION, MOUNT TABOR, ISRAEL

For I am not ashamed of the gospel of Christ,
for it is the power of God to salvation for everyone who believes …

ROMANS 1:16

Journey of Philip

Great people are ordinary people with an extraordinary amount of determination. One such person was Philip the evangelist. The word "evangelist" literally means "one who proclaims good tidings," and although all the disciples of Jesus did this (Acts 8:4), Philip was the only person specifically referred to in the Bible as an evangelist.

He was not the same Philip who was one of the twelve apostles of Christ; he was one of seven men chosen later by all the disciples because he was "full of the Spirit and wisdom." There had been complaints that widows were being overlooked, so these seven were to ensure that there was a fair and equitable distribution when everything was shared among the believers (see Acts 6:1–6).

Although chosen for that ministry, Philip became well known for his evangelism. We could rightly call him the first cross-cultural missionary. When persecution began against the church in Jerusalem, he left the city and went to the city of Samaria, where he brought great joy by proclaiming Christ with many miracles of physical and spiritual healing.

Our ministries may change over time. Being willing to follow the leading of the Holy Spirit is like setting our sails to move with the wind—we don't know where the wind comes from or where it will take us, but we will not be stationary, either as sailors or as Christians moved by the Spirit of God.

Dare to go where no one else has gone. ROBERT H. SCHULLER

SAINT STEPHEN'S OR LION GATE, JERUSALEM, ISRAEL
Stephen is said to have been stoned near this place.

Philip and Stephen were chosen by the early church to be part of a group of seven disciples with special authority. Both were chosen because they were "men full of faith and of the Holy Spirit" (Acts 6:5), and in the near future God would do great works and miraculous signs through them. Philip would have known Stephen well.

Stephen did great wonders that resulted in jealousy among those who wanted to bring him down. These people brought false accusations against Stephen before the high priest of the Sanhedrin. Stephen's fearless courage in the face of his accusers was outstanding, and his Christ-like forgiveness of those who were stoning him to death is an example to all who earnestly want to follow in the footsteps of Jesus. We too can forgive our enemies when we are full of faith and of the Holy Spirit.

Philip would most likely have been in Jerusalem at the time of Stephen's stoning or if not he would have heard about it. Philip and many of the disciples left soon after to go and spread the Good News about Jesus, so nothing was going to stop them.

For God has not given us a spirit of fear, but of power and of love and of a sound mind. Therefore do not be ashamed of the testimony of our Lord, nor of me His prisoner, but share with me in the sufferings for the gospel according to the power of God, who has saved us and called us with a holy calling, not according to our works, but according to His own purpose and grace which was given to us in Christ Jesus before time began, but has now been revealed by the appearing of our Savior Jesus Christ, who has abolished death and brought life and immortality to light through the gospel...

2 TIMOTHY 1:7–10

THE TEMPLE MOUNT, JERUSALEM, LOOKING EAST
This is the area where Solomon's temple was located. Philip, Stephen and the other disciples would have spent a lot of time here because it was a meeting place.

God gives endurance to match encounters. ROBERT H. SCHULLER

JACOB'S WELL, SYCHAR, SAMARIA (NABLUS).
Philip would have been well aware of the remarkable effect Jesus had on a Samaritan woman who gave Him water at this well, and it is probable that Philip also went to this well while in Samaria. The well is now protected by the "Church of Jacob's Well" that has been built over it. This well was dug by Jacob (a patriarch of the faith) over 3000 years ago, yet the water today is still as clear and fresh as in Jesus' day.

Then Philip went down to the city of Samaria and preached Christ to them. And the multitudes with one accord heeded the things spoken by Philip, hearing and seeing the miracles which he did. For unclean spirits, crying with a loud voice, came out of many who were possessed; and many who were paralyzed and lame were healed. And there was great joy in that city … when they believed Philip as he preached the things concerning the kingdom of God and the name of Jesus Christ, both men and women were baptized … Now when the apostles who were at Jerusalem heard that Samaria had received the word of God, they sent Peter and John to them, who, when they had come down, prayed for them that they might receive the Holy Spirit. For as yet He had fallen upon none of them. They had only been baptized in the name of the Lord Jesus. Then they laid hands on them, and they received the Holy Spirit.

ACTS 8:5–17

MOSQUE, EIN AL DERWEH, PALESTINE
This mosque is near the well where it is believed Philip baptized the Ethiopian eunuch, on the road to Gaza.

Now an angel of the Lord spoke to Philip, saying, "Arise and go toward the south along the road which goes down from Jerusalem to Gaza." This is desert. So he arose and went. And behold, a man of Ethiopia, a eunuch of great authority under Candace the queen of the Ethiopians, who had charge of all her treasury, and had come to Jerusalem to worship, was returning. And sitting in his chariot, he was reading Isaiah the prophet. Then the Spirit said to Philip, "Go near and overtake this chariot."

So Philip ran to him, and heard him reading the prophet Isaiah, and said, "Do you understand what you are reading?" And he said, "How can I, unless someone guides me?" And he asked Philip to come up and sit with him. The place in the Scripture which he read was this:

"He was led as a sheep to the slaughter;
And as a lamb before its shearer is silent,
So He opened not His mouth.
In His humiliation His justice was taken away,
And who will declare His generation?
For His life is taken from the earth."

So the eunuch answered Philip and said, "I ask you, of whom does the prophet say this, of himself or of some other man?"

Then Philip opened his mouth, and beginning at this Scripture, preached Jesus to him. Now as they went down the road, they came to some water. And the eunuch said, "See, here is water. What hinders me from being baptized?" Then Philip said, "If you believe with all your heart, you may."

And he answered and said, "I believe that Jesus Christ is the Son of God."

So he commanded the chariot to stand still. And both Philip and the eunuch went down into the water, and he baptized him. Now when they came up out of the water, the Spirit of the Lord caught Philip away, so that the eunuch saw him no more; and he went on his way rejoicing. ACTS 8:26–39

Look for the light behind every shadow. ROBERT H. SCHULLER

OLIVE PRESS, BETOGABRI, ISRAEL

Philip may have enjoyed oil from this very press as he would have passed through this area.

We are hard-pressed on every side, yet not crushed; we are perplexed, but not in despair; persecuted, but not forsaken; struck down, but not destroyed—always carrying about in the body the dying of the Lord Jesus, that the life of Jesus also may be manifested in our body.

2 CORINTHIANS 4:8–10

Be anxious for nothing, but in everything by prayer and supplication, with thanksgiving, let your requests be made known to God; and the peace of God, which surpasses all understanding, will guard your hearts and minds through Christ Jesus.

PHILIPPIANS 4:6–7

Olive presses were a common sight in the apostle Paul's day. After olive oil was extracted from the fruit, it was not only used in food preparation, but also as fuel for lamps, as anointing oil, and for dressing wounds. The diet of the occupying Romans also included olives and olive oil.

Some of the words Paul used in his second letter to the church in Corinth (opposite page), may well have been written with the image of an olive press in his mind: "we are hard-pressed on every side . . ."

The branches of fruit-bearing olive trees were beaten with sticks, and the fallen fruit collected. This may also have been in Paul's mind when he wrote, "we are . . . struck down, but not destroyed."

Olive oil, mixed with spices and sweet-smelling herbs, became expensively perfumed ointments, which were often used ceremonially and symbolically.

Jesus was moved when Mary poured an expensive ointment on His head. He defended her extravagant gesture, saying to her critics, "Why do you trouble her? She has done a good work for Me . . . She has done what she could. She has come beforehand to anoint My body for burial." (See Mark 14:6–8)

Not long after that occasion, Jesus was in the Garden of *Gethsemane*, knowing He was facing imminent death. Gethsemane is thought to be in an olive grove located on the Mount of Olives. The word Gethsemane is a transliteration of the Hebrew/Aramaic for "olive press."

OLIVE CRUSHER, ANCIENT RUINS NEAR BETOGOBRI, ISRAEL

CRUSADER SEA FORT, AZOTUS, ISRAEL

Azotus was known as Ashdod in Old Testaments times. This castle was built in the area where an older city existed at the time of Philip. Stones from the old buildings were used in this building.

... the Spirit of the Lord caught Philip away, so that the eunuch saw him no more; and he went on his way rejoicing. But Philip was found at Azotus. And passing through, he preached in all the cities till he came to Caesarea. ACTS 8:39–40

JAFFA BEACH (ANCIENT JOPPA), ISRAEL

Like tides that are subject to the gravitational attraction of the moon and the sun, the gospel goes out, subject to the power of the Holy Spirit, gravitating around the attraction of the Son, and bringing glory to God, our Creator and Redeemer.

Too often, we are like children who play with small things on a beach while the vast ocean of God's love laps around us, unnoticed in our trifling play.

Only occasionally do we pause, reflect, and then joyfully drown in that ocean of love and grace, becoming part of the waves that wash into the lives of others, bringing blessing and peace.

Have you not known?
Have you not heard?
The everlasting God, the Lord,
The Creator of the ends of the earth,
Neither faints nor is weary.
His understanding is unsearchable.
He gives power to the weak,
And to those who have no might He increases strength.
Even the youths shall faint and be weary,
And the young men shall utterly fall,
But those who wait on the Lord
Shall renew their strength;
They shall mount up with wings like eagles,
They shall run and not be weary,
They shall walk and not faint.

ISAIAH 40:28–31

CRUSADER FORT, ANTIPATRIS, ISRAEL

This fort is built on the ruins of the city that existed at the time of Philip. Antipatris was a Roman military post on the Roman road between Jerusalem and Caesarea. It was built by Herod the Great. The Roman soldiers who transported the apostle Paul as a prisoner lodged in Antipatris before presenting Paul before Felix, the governor of Judea. (See Acts 23:31)

God's care will carry you so you can carry others! ROBERT H. SCHULLER

THE MARTYRIUM OF SAINT PHILIP, HIERAPOLIS, TURKEY

There is some confusion over whether it was the apostle Philip or Philip the evangelist who was crucified on this location, known today as Pamukkale. Whoever it was, the church was built over the place said to hold the remains of Philip.

What then shall we say to these things? If God is for us, who can be against us? He who did not spare His own Son, but delivered Him up for us all, how shall He not with Him also freely give us all things? Who shall bring a charge against God's elect? It is God who justifies. Who is he who condemns? It is Christ who died, and furthermore is also risen, who is even at the right hand of God, who also makes intercession for us. Who shall separate us from the love of Christ? Shall tribulation, or distress, or persecution, or famine, or nakedness, or peril, or sword? As it is written: "For Your sake we are killed all day long; We are accounted as sheep for the slaughter." Yet in all these things we are more than conquerors through Him who loved us. For I am persuaded that neither death nor life, nor angels nor principalities nor powers, nor things present nor things to come, nor height nor depth, nor any other created thing, shall be able to separate us from the love of God which is in Christ Jesus our Lord.

ROMANS 8:31–39

Jesus said ... "I am the light of the world. He who follows Me shall not walk in darkness, but have the light of life."

JOHN 8:12

FRONTINUS GATE, HIERAPOLIS, TURKEY

The gate was named after its builder, Julius Frontinus, the Asian proconsul A.D. 84–86, and dedicated to the Roman emperor Domitian. This is the main road, so Philip would have walked on these very stones while in this area.

Thoughts are like roads; you never know where they will lead you. ROBERT H. SCHULLER

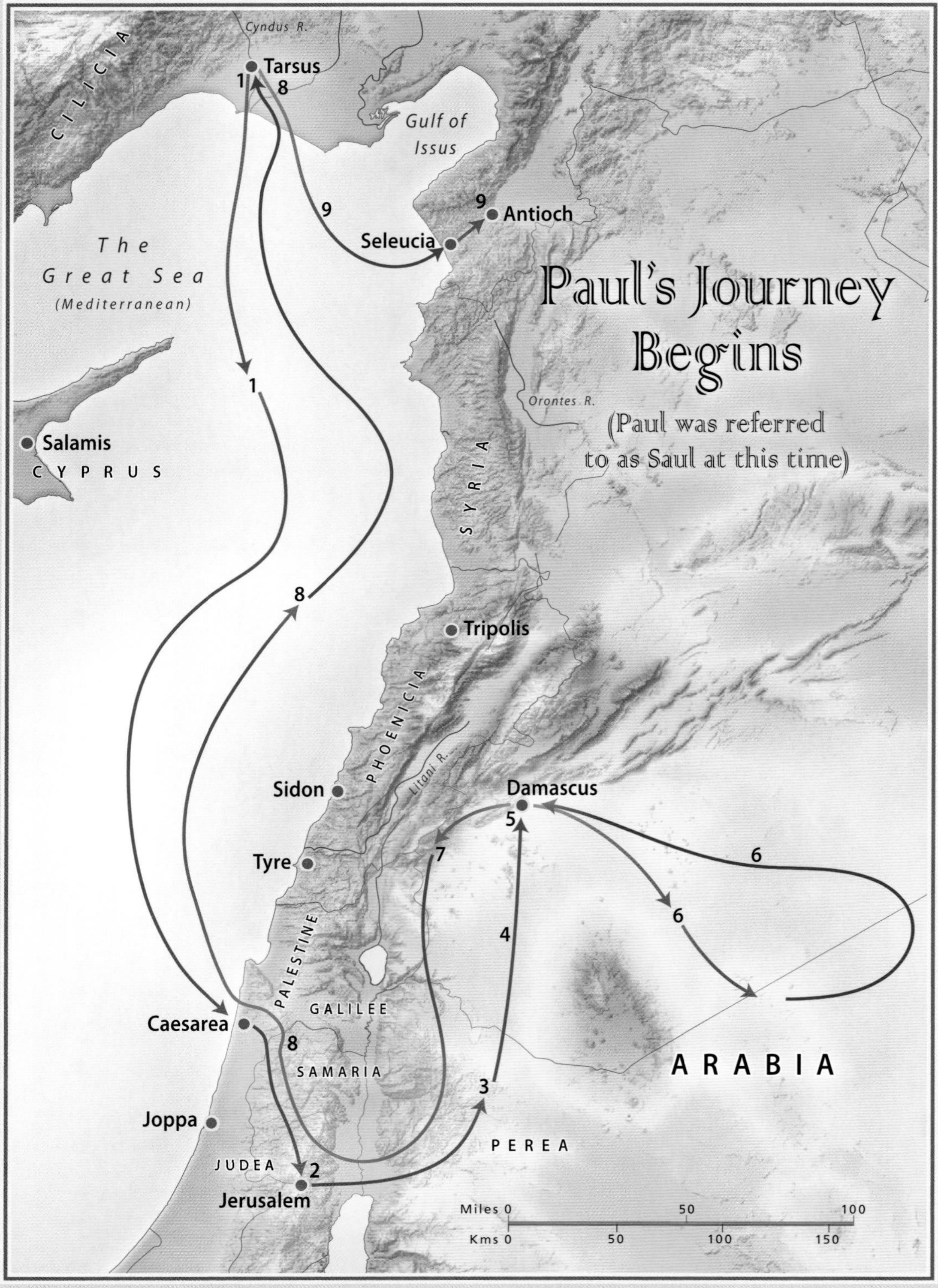

KEY

1. Saul sails from Tarsus to Caesarea, then travels to Jerusalem to study. Acts 22:3

2. Saul is at the stoning of Stephen. Acts 7:58–8:1

3. Leaving Jerusalem, Saul travels on the road to Damascus.

4. Saul's conversion on the road to Damascus. Acts 9:3–6

5. Saul meets Ananias at Straight Street in Damascus. Acts 9:11–16
Saul spends time with Ananias and the disciples. Acts 9:17–20
Saul escapes from Damascus in a basket. Acts 9:25

6. He spends time in Arabia, then returns to Damascus. Galatians1:17

7. Back to Jerusalem. Galatians 1:18

8. From Jerusalem to Caesarea and on to Tarsus. Acts 9:29–30

9. Saul goes to Antioch and preaches. Acts 11:25–26

Lines show only general direction and approximate sequence of journeys.

To farthest point

From farthest point

● Generally accepted or known location

SAUL FALLING FROM HIS HORSE, ANANIAS' HOUSE, DAMASCUS, SYRIA

...deliver us from the evil one.
For Yours is the kingdom and the power and the glory forever...

MATTHEW 6:13

ACTS OF THE APOSTLES

Paul's Journey Begins

He had approved the stoning to death of Stephen (Acts 6), and now, "breathing out murderous threats," Saul of Tarsus was on the road to Damascus with the necessary documentation to arrest followers of the Way. He would take them as prisoners to Jerusalem where they would undoubtedly suffer Stephen's fate.

The life of Saul, a first-century terrorist, was changed forever when he encountered the resurrected Jesus Christ. Blinded for three days by a light from heaven, Saul fell to the ground. Questioned and then commanded by the voice of Jesus, Saul was speechless.

Sometimes we need to be brought down from our high horses before we can identify the voice of Jesus speaking to us—through the words of Scripture, through a friend who believes in Him, through the glory of God's creation, or perhaps in a time of trauma.

When Saul obeyed the Lord and went to the house of Ananias in Damascus, this former persecutor of Christians was filled with the Holy Spirit and immediately began preaching in the synagogues that Jesus is the Son of God. No longer on his high horse, Saul became a humble, transformed man. Even the hardest heart will be softened after an encounter with Jesus. He went on to be one of the greatest ambassadors for Jesus.

God's miraculous timing for my life is perfect! ROBERT H. SCHULLER

THE TRIUMPHAL ARCH OF SERVUS ON THE OLD ROMAN ROAD, TARSUS, TURKEY

Tarsus was a university city, a commercial center and the chief city of the Roman province of Cilicia. Situated in a fertile valley, it lay near the only good trade route between Asia Minor and Syria, so it was a wealthy city. Black goats were plentiful in Paul's childhood home of Tarsus, and their hair was woven into fabric to make tents and saddles.

WILD POPPIES ALONG OLD ROMAN ROAD, TARSUS

You are God's project and God never fails. ROBERT H. SCHULLER

CAESAREA HARBOR, ISRAEL Located between modern Haifa and Jerusalem, Caesarea featured prominently in the life of Paul. It was his port of call after missionary journeys; he was sent here for trial, spent two years here in prison, and finally sailed from this harbor in chains to make his appeal before the emperor in Rome.

...both in my chains and in the ... confirmation of the gospel, you all are partakers with me of grace. PHILIPPIANS 1:7

God will have the last word and it will be good. ROBERT H. SCHULLER

SAINT STEPHEN'S CHURCH, KIDRON VALLEY, JERUSALEM, ISRAEL

This is the old Roman area where Stephen was stoned to death.

Stephen said to the religious leaders who falsely accused him: "You stiff-necked and uncircumcised in heart and ears! You always resist the Holy Spirit; as your fathers did, so do you. Which of the prophets did your fathers not persecute? And they killed those who foretold the coming of the Just One, of whom you now have become the betrayers and murderers, who have received the law by the direction of angels and have not kept it."

When they heard these things they were cut to the heart, and they gnashed at him with their teeth. But he, being full of the Holy Spirit, gazed into heaven and saw the glory of God, and Jesus standing at the right hand of God, and said, "Look! I see the heavens opened and the Son of Man standing at the right hand of God!" Then they cried out with a loud voice, stopped their ears, and ran at him with one accord; and they cast him out of the city and stoned him. And the witnesses laid down their clothes at the feet of a young man named Saul. And they stoned Stephen as he was calling on God and saying, "Lord Jesus, receive my spirit." Then he knelt down and cried out with a loud voice, "Lord, do not charge them with this sin." And when he had said this, he fell asleep.

ACTS 7:51–60

One of those involved with Stephen's stoning was Saul, a persecutor of the Christians. Saul, who was later named Paul, became one of the greatest apostles of all. Maybe seeing the reality of Stephen's faith and his ability to forgive those who were stoning him to death helped prepare Paul for his own life-transforming encounter with the risen Jesus.

STONING OF STEPHEN FRESCO, SAINT STEPHEN'S CHURCH, KIDRON VALLEY, JERUSALEM

Saul was watching as Stephen was stoned to death.

Success without conflict is unrealistic. ROBERT H. SCHULLER

DAMASCUS GATE, JERUSALEM, ISRAEL

Then Saul, still breathing threats and murder against the disciples of the Lord, went to the high priest and asked letters from him to the synagogues of Damascus, so that if he found any who were of the Way, whether men or women, he might bring them bound to Jerusalem.

As he journeyed he came near Damascus, and suddenly a light shone around him from heaven. Then he fell to the ground, and heard a voice saying to him, "Saul, Saul, why are you persecuting Me?"

And he said, "Who are You, Lord?"

Then the Lord said, "I am Jesus, whom you are persecuting. It is hard for you to kick against the goads."

So he, trembling and astonished, said, "Lord, what do You want me to do?"

Then the Lord said to him, "Arise and go into the city, and you will be told what you must do."

And the men who journeyed with him stood speechless, hearing a voice but seeing no one. Then Saul arose from the ground, and when his eyes were opened he saw no one. But they led him by the hand and brought him into Damascus. And he was three days without sight, and neither ate nor drank.

ACTS 8:26–39

SAINT PAUL'S CHURCH, KAUKAB, SYRIA

This area is thought to be where Saul fell off his horse and heard the voice of Jesus.

The path of humility is the path to glory. ROBERT H. SCHULLER

STRAIGHT STREET, BOUSRA Paul probably came through Bousra before falling off his horse. This city was on the main Roman road leading to Damascus.

Turn your stumbling block into a stepping stone. ROBERT H. SCHULLER

STRAIGHT STREET, DAMASCUS, SYRIA

This was the name given to any route in antiquity that extended straight through a city. Damascus is one of the oldest continuously occupied towns in the world.

Now there was a certain disciple at Damascus named Ananias; and to him the Lord said in a vision, "Ananias."

And he said, "Here I am, Lord."

So the Lord said to him, "Arise and go to the street called Straight, and inquire at the house of Judas for one called Saul of Tarsus, for behold, he is praying. And in a vision he has seen a man named Ananias coming in and putting his hand on him, so that he might receive his sight."

Then Ananias answered, "Lord, I have heard from many about this man, how much harm he has done to Your saints in Jerusalem. And here he has authority from the chief priests to bind all who call on Your name."

But the Lord said to him, "Go, for he is a chosen vessel of Mine to bear My name before Gentiles, kings, and the children of Israel.

ACTS 9:10–15

Ananias went his way and entered the house; and laying his hands on him he said, "Brother Saul, the Lord Jesus, who appeared to you on the road as you came, has sent me that you may receive your sight and be filled with the Holy Spirit." Immediately there fell from his eyes something like scales, and he received his sight at once; and he arose and was baptized.

So when he had received food, he was strengthened. Then Saul spent some days with the disciples at Damascus. Immediately he preached the Christ in the synagogues, that He is the Son of God.

ACTS 9:17–20

SAINT ANANIAS' CHURCH, DAMASCUS, SYRIA

It is believed that this was the location and part of the house where Ananias placed his hands on Saul, healing him of blindness. Saul was filled with the Holy Spirit at this point. (See Acts 9:17)

Lord, make my life a window for your light to shine through. ROBERT H. SCHULLER

SAINT PAUL'S GATE, DAMASCUS, SYRIA

This is part of ancient Damascus where it is believed Paul (still referred to as Saul) was lowered in a basket over the city wall.

SAINT ANANIAS' CHURCH, DAMASCUS, SYRIA

A painted carving depicting Paul's escape from the city.

Now after many days were past, the Jews plotted to kill him. But their plot became known to Saul. And they watched the gates day and night, to kill him. Then the disciples took him by night and let him down through the wall in a large basket.

ACTS 9:23–25

SUNRISE, MOUNT KASSION, OVERLOOKING DAMASCUS, SYRIA

It is believed that Cain killed Abel on this mountain. This is certainly a place Paul would have seen during his time in Damascus.

Trying times are times to try-UMPH! ROBERT H. SCHULLER

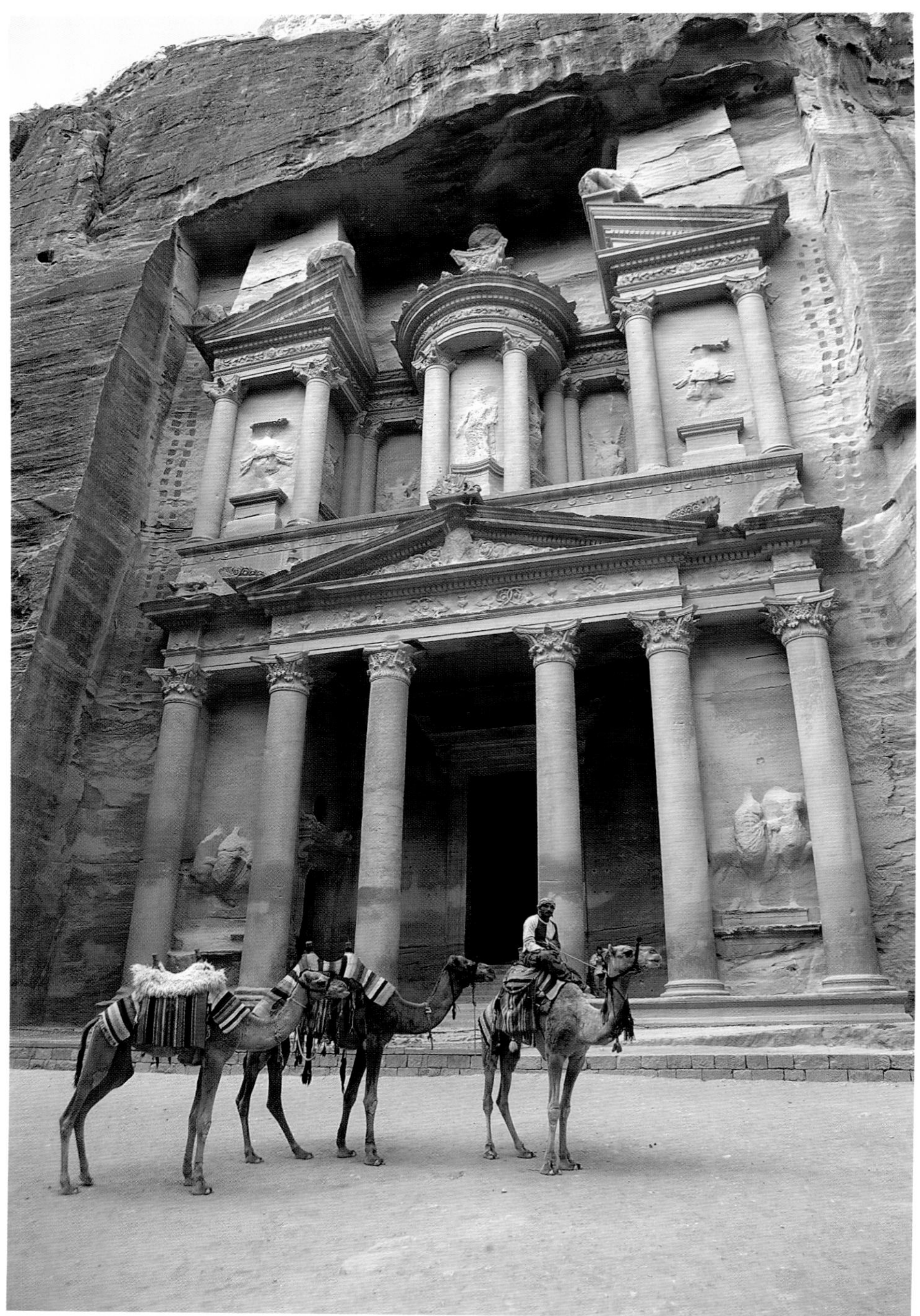

TREASURY BUILDING, PETRA, JORDAN

Tradition holds that this is where Saul spent time when he went to Arabia not long after receiving his vision of Jesus. (See Galatians 1:15–17)

"Time-out" is a colloquial expression today and usually means to make a time to physically and emotionally retreat from the daily routine. It seems logical, considering the trauma of Saul's recent encounter with the risen Christ, that he should want time-out. Time to reflect on his radical transformation; the overwhelming new paradigm that defined his life, his entire belief system; his view of history and of the future.

Time to humbly gain strength to go out and face the present realities of an existence where he would no longer be the famously murderous persecutor, but one of God's persecuted people, gladly proclaiming the good news of His salvation for all.

For you have heard of my former conduct in Judaism, how I persecuted the church of God beyond measure and tried to destroy it. And I advanced in Judaism beyond many of my contemporaries in my own nation, being more exceedingly zealous for the traditions of my fathers. But when it pleased God, who separated me from my mother's womb and called me through His grace, to reveal His Son in me, that I might preach Him among the Gentiles, I did not immediately confer with flesh and blood, nor did I go up to Jerusalem to those who were apostles before me; but I went to Arabia, and returned again to Damascus.

GALATIANS 1:13–17

SIQ GORGE, ENTRY INTO PETRA, JORDAN

What a beautiful place to go and spend time growing in knowledge of God!

No one emerges from a problem untouched by tough times. But you have managed to turn your hurts into halos and your scars into stars! ROBERT H. SCHULLER

TARSUS (BERDAN) FALLS, TARSUS, TURKEY
Paul probably saw this area as it is the main water source for Tarsus.

And when Saul had come to Jerusalem, he tried to join the disciples; but they were all afraid of him, and did not believe that he was a disciple. But Barnabas took him and brought him to the apostles. And he declared to them how he had seen the Lord on the road, and that He had spoken to him, and how he had preached boldly at Damascus in the name of Jesus. So he was with them at Jerusalem, coming in and going out. And he spoke boldly in the name of the Lord Jesus and disputed against the Hellenists, but they attempted to kill him. When the brethren found out, they brought him down to Caesarea and sent him out to Tarsus.

ACTS 9:26–30

Then Barnabas departed for Tarsus to seek Saul. And when he had found him, he brought him to Antioch. So it was that for a whole year they assembled with the church and taught a great many people. And the disciples were first called Christians in Antioch.

ACTS 11:25–26

THE SEA WALL TO OLD PORT, SELEUCIA, TURKEY
Seleucia was the closest Roman port to Antioch. It would have been the port that Saul, Barnabas, and many early Christians would have come to if sailing to Antioch.

Success is not measured by what you've done. It's measured by who you've become. ROBERT H. SCHULLER

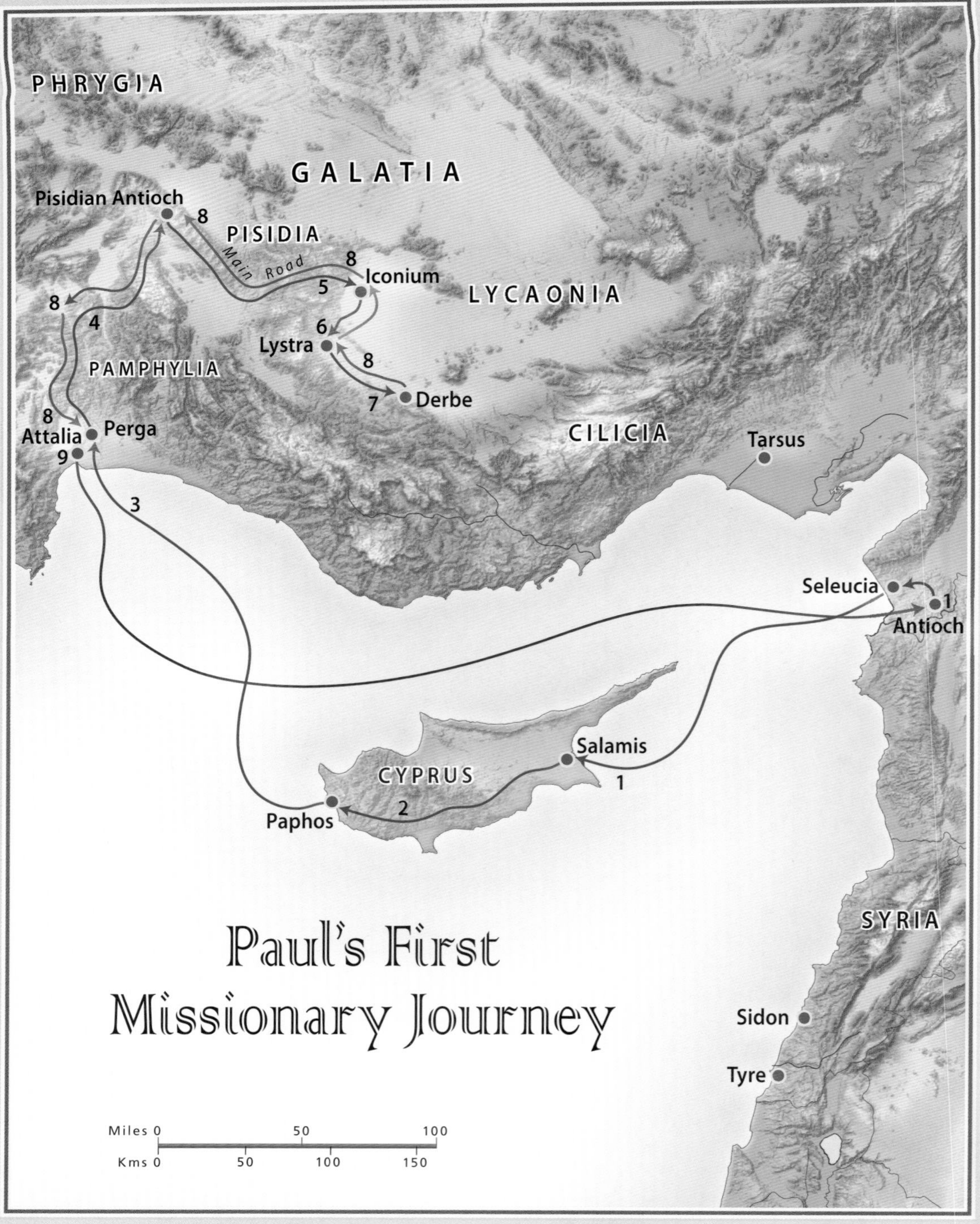

KEY

1. From Antioch to Seleucia then by ship to Salamis, Cyprus. Acts 13:2–5

2. Paul travels to Paphos, Cyprus. Acts 13:5–6
Saul is referred to now as Paul. Acts 13:9
A sorcerer is blinded by Paul. Acts 3:6–12

3. Leaves Paphos and goes to Perga in Pamphylia. Acts 13:13

4. From Perga to Pisidian Antioch. Acts13:14
Paul preaches at Pisidian Antioch. Acts13:16–41

5. From Pisidian Antioch Paul goes to Iconium. Acts 13:50–51

6. Paul goes to Lystra and is stoned. Acts 14:5–19

7. Paul goes to Derbe and preaches to believers. Acts 14:20–21

8. Paul returns through Lystra, Iconium, Pisidian Antioch, and Perga. Churches begin in these places. Acts 14:21–25

9. From Perga Paul goes to Attalia. Acts 14:25

10. Paul returns to Antioch in Syria. Acts 14:26–28

Lines show only general direction and approximate sequence of journeys.

→ To farthest point

→ From farthest point

● Generally accepted or known location

ICON OF SAINT PAUL, SAINT PAUL'S CHURCH, KALIO LIMENES, CRETE
Located in the vicinity of Fair Havens, where Paul took shelter.

Your word is a lamp to my feet and a light to my path.

PSALM 119:105

Paul's First Missionary Journey

The Christian church was born when the Holy Spirit was poured out on a group of disciples gathered in prayer. Now, about ten years after Ananias had laid hands on blind Saul and he had been filled with the Holy Spirit, this transformed persecutor was chosen and sent out by the Holy Spirit while he fasted and prayed with a group of disciples.

Paul's first missionary journey did not begin because of a carefully planned and researched strategy; it began with submission to God in prayer and fasting, a time when the Lord's people then, and now, seem most sensitive to the leading of His Holy Spirit.

How good to know, even before he set out; before he met Elymas the sorcerer; before he preached in the synagogue in Pisidian Antioch; before he was worshipped and then stoned in Lystra, that Paul's journey was not the plan of man but of God's Holy Spirit.

We do not know who will be called and sent out by God, but we do know that time spent with Him in prayer is never a waste of time. Prayer prepares us for the journey ahead.

Winning starts with beginning! ROBERT H. SCHULLER

OLIVE TREES, ANTIOCH, TURKEY

...remember that you do not support the root, but the root supports you. ROMANS 11:18

A GYMNASIUM IN THE ARCHEOLOGICAL RUINS IN SALAMIS, CYPRUS

As they ministered to the Lord and fasted, the Holy Spirit said, "Now separate to Me Barnabas and Saul for the work to which I have called them." Then, having fasted and prayed, and laid hands on them, they sent them away. So, being sent out by the Holy Spirit, they went down to Seleucia, and from there they sailed to Cyprus. And when they arrived in Salamis, they preached the word of God in the synagogues of the Jews.

ACTS 13:2–5

SAINT BARNABAS' TOMB, SAINT BARNABAS MONASTERY, NEAR SALAMIS, CYPRUS

According to tradition, Barnabas was martyred here during the reign of Nero.

ICON OF SAINT BARNABAS BEING STONED, SAINT BARNABAS MONASTERY, NEAR SALAMIS, CYPRUS.

The name Barnabas means 'Son of Encouragement.' According to Acts, Barnabas gave financially to those in need in the church (4:36–37). It was Barnabas who introduced the former persecutor, Paul, to the disciples in Jerusalem, who were still afraid of him (9:27). Barnabas really was an encourager of the faith and appears to be the sort of person who didn't care who got the credit, as long as he was serving God with all that he had. God can really do great things through a person with a humble heart!

Once you've committed to a goal, the power will begin to flow into your life. ROBERT H. SCHULLER

SAINT LAZARUS' CHURCH, LARNACA (ANCIENT KITION), CYPRUS
It is believed that the first bishop in this church was Lazarus and that his tomb is located here.

Early Christian tradition held that Lazarus sought refuge in Kition, Cyprus, after being persecuted by the high priests and Pharisees in Jerusalem. It is probable that he left Jerusalem with the other disciples who dispersed after the stoning of Stephen. It is believed that he met Paul and Barnabas on their missionary journeys and was ordained by them as the first bishop of Kition.

SAINT LAZARUS' CHURCH, LARNACA, CYPRUS
The skull framed in this ornate receptacle is thought to belong to Lazarus.

Truly, one person can make a difference! ROBERT H. SCHULLER

Legend has it that Aphrodite was born of the sea foam near Paphos, Cyprus. She was the classical Greek goddess of love, sex, and beauty, and her chief center of worship was at Paphos.

Sexual immorality has always been a trap, and it's interesting that one of the places Paul visited first on his missionary trips was Paphos, a place where the worship of sex and lust was taken for granted. Paul not only resisted the seduction of false gods, he also demonstrated that walking with Jesus brings the power to transform lives and old habits. It was in this region of many gods that Paul and Barnabas insisted that the people should turn from these useless things to a living God, who made the heaven, the earth, the sea, and all that is in them.

For this, Paul was stoned. It didn't stop him returning to this region later to encourage those who had believed the message and had joyfully turned away from the worship of lifeless gods.

APHRODITE'S BIRTHPLACE, NEAR PAPHOS, CYPRUS

... the Gentiles begged that these words might be preached to them ... ACTS 13:42

When you discover the beauty in yourself, you will begin to discover the beauty in others. ROBERT H. SCHULLER

CHURCH OF CHRYSOPOLITISSA, PAPHOS, CYPRUS

The white pillar in the foreground is called Saint Paul's Pillar. According to tradition, Paul was tied up and whipped on this spot. We often think we are hard done by when someone offends us. Contemplating what the early apostles suffered and what Jesus Himself endured helps put things in perspective. Paul's love was such that even though he was whipped he continued loving people.

Now when they had gone … to Paphos, they found a certain sorcerer … whose name was Bar-Jesus, who was with the proconsul, Sergius Paulus, an intelligent man. This man called for Barnabas and Saul and sought to hear the word of God. But Elymas the sorcerer (for so his name is translated) withstood them, seeking to turn the proconsul away from the faith. Then Saul, who also is called Paul, filled with the Holy Spirit, looked intently at him and said, "O full of all deceit and all fraud, you son of the devil, you enemy of all righteousness, will you not cease perverting the straight ways of the Lord? And now, indeed, the hand of the Lord is upon you, and you shall be blind, not seeing the sun for a time." And immediately a dark mist fell on him, and he went around seeking someone to lead him by the hand. Then the proconsul believed, when he saw what had been done, being astonished at the teaching of the Lord.

ACTS 13:6–12

MOSAIC FROM THE HOUSE OF THESEUS, PAPHOS, CYPRUS

This house is said to have belonged to Sergius Paulus, a Roman proconsul who became a Christian after Paul's display of power against Elymas, the sorcerer. The powers of the proconsuls were unlimited in both the military and civil areas.

Tune-in to God and tune-in on life. ROBERT H. SCHULLER

ANCIENT DWELLING, PERGA (CAPITAL OF PAMPHYLIA), TURKEY

This dwelling overlooks the main center of Perga. It is believed that Paul preached in this house. It is now sometimes used by shepherds for their sheep.

The Lord is my shepherd;
I shall not want.
He makes me to lie down in green pastures;
He leads me beside the still waters.
He restores my soul;
He leads me in the paths of righteousness
For His name's sake.

Yea, though I walk through the valley
of the shadow of death,
I will fear no evil;
For You are with me;
Your rod and Your staff, they comfort me.

You prepare a table before me
in the presence of my enemies;
You anoint my head with oil;
My cup runs over.
Surely goodness and mercy shall follow me
All the days of my life;
And I will dwell in the house of the Lord
Forever.

PSALM 23:1–6

Now when Paul and his party set sail from Paphos, they came to Perga in Pamphylia; and John, departing from them, returned to Jerusalem.

ACTS 13:13

THE AQUEDUCT, ASPENDOS, NEAR PERGA, TURKEY
This was on the Roman road leading to Pisidian Antioch, which Paul visited.

A big achievement is made up of little steps. ROBERT H. SCHULLER

PAUL PREACHED AT PISIDIAN ANTIOCH, TURKEY

"...if you have any word of exhortation for the people, say on." ACTS 13:15

... in Iconium ... they went together to the synagogue of the Jews, and so spoke that a great multitude both of the Jews and of the Greeks believed. But the unbelieving Jews stirred up the Gentiles and poisoned their minds against the brethren. Therefore they stayed there a long time, speaking boldly in the Lord, who was bearing witness to the word of His grace, granting signs and wonders to be done by their hands. But the multitude of the city was divided: part sided with the Jews, and part with the apostles. And when a violent attempt was made by both the Gentiles and Jews, with their rulers, to abuse and stone them, they became aware of it and fled to Lystra and Derbe, cities of Lycaonia, and to the surrounding region. And they were preaching the gospel there.

ACTS 14:1–7

ICONIUM, TURKEY

Iconium was a major city in the Roman province of Galatia. It is now known as Konia.

... the disciples were filled with joy and with the Holy Spirit. ACTS 13:52

There is no life without growth. ROBERT H. SCHULLER

THE TELL OF THE ANCIENT CITY OF LYSTRA, TURKEY
A tell is a large mound of dirt and debris that collects over time as people build new on top of the old. The tell of Lystra has not yet been excavated.

. . . in Lystra a certain man . . . a cripple from his mother's womb . . . heard Paul speaking. Paul, observing him intently and seeing that he had faith to be healed, said with a loud voice, "Stand up straight on your feet!" And he leaped and walked.

Now when the people saw what Paul had done, they raised their voices, saying in the Lycaonian language, "The gods have come down to us in the likeness of men!" And Barnabas they called Zeus, and Paul, Hermes, because he was the chief speaker. Then the priest of Zeus, whose temple was in front of their city, brought oxen and garlands to the gates, intending to sacrifice with the multitudes.

But when the apostles Barnabas and Paul heard this, they tore their clothes and ran in among the multitude, crying out and saying, "Men, why are you doing these things? We also are men with the same nature as you, and preach to you that you should turn from these useless things to the living God, who made the heaven, the earth, the sea, and all things that are in them, who in bygone generations allowed all nations to walk in their own ways. Nevertheless He did not leave Himself without witness, in that He did good, gave us rain from heaven and fruitful seasons, filling our hearts with food and gladness." And with these sayings they could scarcely restrain the multitudes from sacrificing to them.

Then Jews from Antioch and Iconium came there; and having persuaded the multitudes, they stoned Paul and dragged him out of the city, supposing him to be dead.

ACTS 14:8–19

TRADITIONAL MUD BRICK FARMHOUSE, DERBE, TURKEY
The construction of this traditional farmhouse in the area of Derbe is the same as that used in the time of Paul. The unexcavated tell of ancient Derbe City is in the background.

... when the disciples gathered around him [Paul], he rose up and went into the city. And the next day he departed with Barnabas to Derbe. And when they had preached the gospel to that city and made many disciples, they returned to Lystra, Iconium, and Antioch ...

ACTS 14:20–21

ANCIENT HARBOR OF ATTALIA, TURKEY
Paul sailed from here when he returned to Seleucia.

... when they had preached the word in Perga, they went down to Attalia. From Attalia they sailed to Antioch, where they had been commended to the grace of God for the work which they had completed. Now when they had come and gathered the church together, they reported all that God had done with them, and that He had opened the door of faith to the Gentiles. So they stayed there a long time with the disciples.

ACTS 14:25–28

This is Corycus Castle, with Maiden's Castle in the background. The arch was an ancient sea door to the castle. According to legend, pirates frequented these waters.

Paul faced many dangers during his lifetime, and in his second letter to the Corinthian church he testified to the fact that he "faced dangers on the sea." Since the Mediterranean was a major trade route and Paul sailed it several times, we may safely assume it was here that he faced dangers on the sea.

Paul also wrote in that letter "once I was stoned"—the traditional Jewish method of execution. The stoning had taken place on this first missionary journey, and when Paul wrote later to the church in Galatia "I bear in my body the marks of the Lord Jesus," he undoubtedly referred to the wounds gained at Lystra on this first journey. Those wounds were probably still fresh scars when Paul sailed in this region, on the way home after an almost year-long journey so memorable that we still talk about it today.

CORYCUS CASTLE, KIZKALESI, TURKEY

Sailing on the growing edge of risk brings triumph when God is at the helm. ROBERT H. SCHULLER

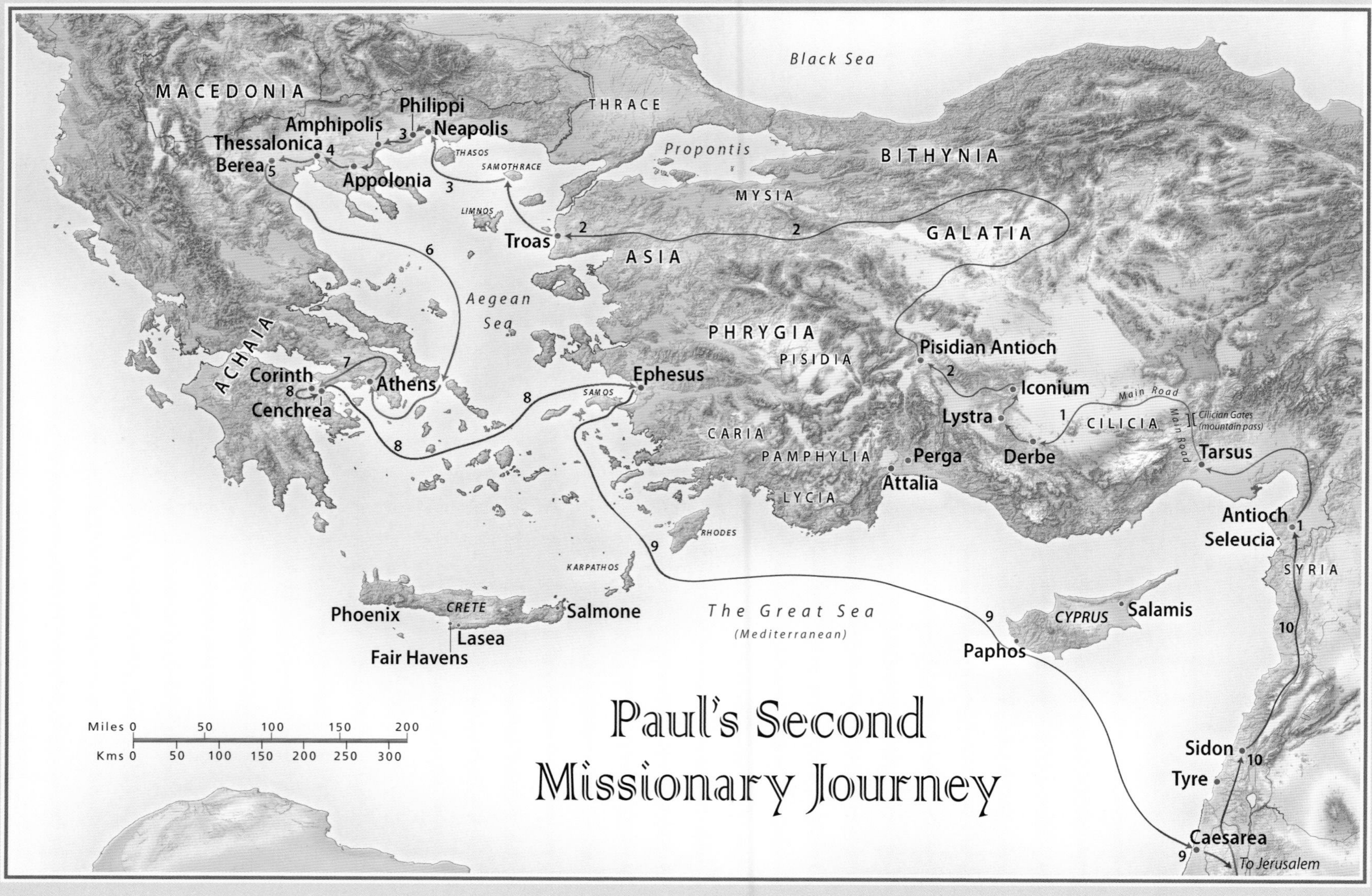

KEY

1. From Antioch Paul and Silas go to Lystra. Acts 15:40–16:1
They meet Timothy there. Acts 16:1–3

2. From Lystra to Troas they strengthen the churches. Acts 16:4–5

3. They depart Troas for Philippi via Neapolis. Acts 16:11–12
Lydia is converted at Philippi. Acts 16:13–15
Paul and Silas are put in prison. Acts 16:24

4. Paul goes to Thessalonica. Acts 16:40–17:1

5. Paul goes to Berea. Acts 17:10–11

6. He leaves Berea for Athens. Acts 17:14–16

7. Paul travels to Corinth. Acts 18:1

8. He goes on to Ephesus via Cenchrea. Acts 18:18–19

9. Paul goes to Jerusalem. Acts 18:21–22

10. After Jerusalem, he goes to Sidon, then to Antioch. Acts 18:22

Lines show only general direction and approximate sequence of journeys.

→ To farthest point

→ From farthest point

● Generally accepted or known location

MOSAIC OF PAUL, CHURCH OF THE HOLY VIRGIN MARY, ANCIENT CORINTH, GREECE

"The Spirit of the Lord *is upon Me,*
Because He has anointed Me
To preach the gospel."

LUKE 4:18

Paul's Second Missionary Journey

Paul's departure on his second journey followed a momentous announcement at the meeting of the church leaders in Jerusalem. The announcement made by the Jerusalem Council was the best news a missionary like Paul could have received. After much deliberation, and much angst on Paul's part, the council had unanimously agreed that the way of salvation and the terms of church fellowship were to be the same for Jews and Gentiles alike; circumcision was not necessary for Gentiles.

Paul and Silas (a leader of the Jerusalem church) were joined by Timothy, a keen young convert from Paul's previous journey. They gladly took with them copies of the momentous decision in Jerusalem to distribute to the growing churches in South Galatia, Syria and Cilicia, and wherever else God led them. The good news of the gospel could be shared with every nation: salvation came by God's grace alone and was to be received through faith in Christ alone.

So Paul began his second journey, again guided by the Spirit of God and with the blessing of the united council of apostles and elders.

His transformation from a persecutor of Christians to a passionate, sensitive, and totally committed Christian who wanted the world to share his faith was nothing short of miraculous.

Lord, be the pilot that guides and controls my life. ROBERT H. SCHULLER

MUD BRICK FARMHOUSE, DERBE, TURKEY
This method of building has not changed since Paul's time. The marble slab on the doorstep was found while the farmer was tilling his fields.

ANCIENT DWELLINGS, KILYSTRA, NEAR LYSTRA, TURKEY

Lystra, a Roman colony, was probably the home of Timothy.

Then he [Paul] came to Derbe and Lystra. And behold, a certain disciple was there, named Timothy, the son of a certain Jewish woman who believed, but his father was Greek. He was well spoken of by the brethren who were at Lystra and Iconium.

ACTS 16:1–2

PISIDIAN ANTIOCH, TURKEY

Farming country on the outskirts of Pisidian Antioch.
Paul would have traveled through this countryside.

Jesus said... What man of you, having a hundred sheep, if he loses one of them, does not leave the ninety-nine in the wilderness, and go after the one which is lost until he finds it? And when he has found it, he lays it on his shoulders, rejoicing. And when he comes home, he calls together his friends and neighbors, saying to them, 'Rejoice with me, for I have found my sheep which was lost!' I say to you that likewise there will be more joy in heaven over one sinner who repents than over ninety-nine just persons who need no repentance.

LUKE 15:4-7

Now when they had gone through Phrygia and the region of Galatia, they were forbidden by the Holy Spirit to preach the word in Asia. After they had come to Mysia, they tried to go into Bithynia, but the Spirit did not permit them. So passing by Mysia, they came down to Troas. And a vision appeared to Paul in the night. A man of Macedonia stood and pleaded with him, saying, "Come over to Macedonia and help us." Now after he had seen the vision, immediately we sought to go to Macedonia, concluding that the Lord had called us to preach the gospel to them. Therefore, sailing from Troas, we ran a straight course to Samothrace, and the next day came to Neapolis, and from there to Philippi, which is the foremost city of that part of Macedonia, a colony. And we were staying in that city for some days.

ACTS 16:6–12

WILD POPPIES NEAR TROAS, TURKEY, OVERLOOKING THE AEGEAN SEA

OLD HARBOR AREA, ALEXANDRIA TROAS, TURKEY

They see the works of the Lord, and His wonders in the deep. PSALM 107:24

MOSAIC IN SAINT NICHOLAS' CHURCH, KAVALA, GREECE
This church is built on the site where it is believed Paul stepped ashore at Neapolis (the ancient name for Kavala). Neapolis was the seaport for Philippi, ten miles away.

ICON OF LYDIA, SAINT PAUL'S CATHEDRAL, KAVALA, GREECE
Lydia was the first convert to Christianity in the whole of Europe.

...on the Sabbath day we went out of the city to the riverside, where prayer was customarily made; and we sat down and spoke to the women who met there. Now a certain woman named Lydia heard us. She was a seller of purple from the city of Thyatira, who worshiped God. The Lord opened her heart to heed the things spoken by Paul. And when she and her household were baptized, she begged us, saying, "If you have judged me to be faithful to the Lord, come to my house and stay." So she persuaded us.

ACTS 16:13–15

PRISON OF PAUL AND SILAS, ARCHEOLOGICAL SITE, PHILIPPI, GREECE

Paul and Silas were thrown into prison (see page 96)

[The jailor] put them into the inner prison and fastened with their feet in stocks. But at midnight Paul and Silas were praying and singing hymns to God, and the prisoners were listening to them. Suddenly there was a great earthquake, so that the foundations of the prison were shaken; and immediately all the doors were opened and everyone's chains were loosed. And the keeper of the prison, awaking from sleep and seeing the prison doors open, supposing the prisoners had fled, drew his sword and was about to kill himself.

But Paul called with a loud voice, saying, "Do yourself no harm, for we are all here."

Then he called for a light, ran in, and fell down trembling before Paul and Silas. And he brought them out and said, "Sirs, what must I do to be saved?"

So they said, "Believe on the Lord Jesus Christ, and you will be saved, you and your household." Then they spoke the word of the Lord to him and to all who were in his house.

And he took them the same hour of the night and washed their stripes. And immediately he and all his family were baptized. Now when he had brought them into his house, he set food before them; and he rejoiced, having believed in God with all his household.

ACTS 16:24–34

Life's not fair but God is good. ROBERT H. SCHULLER

Now it happened, as we went to prayer, that a certain slave girl possessed with a spirit of divination met us, who brought her masters much profit by fortune-telling. This girl followed Paul and us, and cried out, saying, "These men are the servants of the Most High God, who proclaim to us the way of salvation." And this she did for many days.

But Paul, greatly annoyed, turned and said to the spirit, "I command you in the name of Jesus Christ to come out of her." And he came out that very hour.

But when her masters saw that their hope of profit was gone, they seized Paul and Silas and dragged them into the marketplace to the authorities. And they brought them to the magistrates, and said, "These men, being Jews, exceedingly trouble our city; and they teach customs which are not lawful for us, being Romans, to receive or observe." Then the multitude rose up together against them; and the magistrates tore off their clothes and commanded them to be beaten with rods. And when they had laid many stripes on them, they threw them into prison, commanding the jailer to keep them securely.

ACTS 16:16–23

ROMAN AGORA, PHILIPPI, GREECE This is where Paul and Silas were tried and flogged.

"If you abide in My word, you are My disciples indeed. And you shall know the truth, and the truth shall make you free." JOHN 8:31–32

God can keep you focused on your goals, despite every injustice in your path. ROBERT H. SCHULLER

FISHERMEN NEAR ANCIENT AMPHIPOLIS Paul would have passed this way on his journey to Thessalonica.

[Jesus] said to them, "Follow Me, and I will make you fishers of men." MATTHEW 4:19

APOLLONIA, GREECE

It is thought that this is where Paul, Silas, and other followers of Jesus spent time in prayer on their way to Thessalonica. It is claimed that this tree dates from Paul's time.

Jesus said . . . "In this manner, therefore, pray:

Our Father in heaven,
Hallowed be Your name.
Your kingdom come.
Your will be done
On earth as it is in heaven.
Give us this day our daily bread.
And forgive us our debts,
As we forgive our debtors.
And do not lead us into temptation,
But deliver us from the evil one.
For Yours is the kingdom and the power and the glory forever. Amen."

MATTHEW 6:9-13

ARCH OF GALERIUS, THESSALONICA, GREECE
The impressive architecture illustrates Roman power.

MONASTERY OF VLATADON, GREECE
Local tradition holds that Paul preached here to the Jews.

Now when they had passed through Amphipolis and Apollonia, they came to Thessalonica, where there was a synagogue of the Jews. Then Paul, as his custom was, went in to them, and for three Sabbaths reasoned with them from the Scriptures, explaining and demonstrating that the Christ had to suffer and rise again from the dead, and saying, "This Jesus whom I preach to you is the Christ." And some of them were persuaded ...

ACTS 17:1–4

... a great multitude of the devout Greeks, and not a few of the leading women, joined Paul and Silas. But the Jews who were not persuaded, becoming envious, took some of the evil men from the marketplace, and gathering a mob, set all the city in an uproar and attacked the house of Jason ... But when they did not find them, they dragged Jason and some brethren to the rulers of the city, crying out, "These who have turned the world upside down have come here too. Jason has harbored them, and these are all acting contrary to the decrees of Caesar, saying there is another king—Jesus."

ACTS 17:4–7

EASTERN BYZANTINE WALLS, THESSALONICA, GREECE

THE APOSTLE PAUL'S ALTAR, VERIA (ANCIENT BEREA), GREECE

It is believed that Paul spoke to the people of Berea from these steps.

Then the brethren immediately sent Paul and Silas away by night to Berea. When they arrived, they went into the synagogue of the Jews. These were more fair-minded than those in Thessalonica, in that they received the word with all readiness, and searched the Scriptures daily to find out whether these things were so. Therefore many of them believed, and also not a few of the Greeks, prominent women as well as men. But when the Jews from Thessalonica learned that the word of God was preached by Paul at Berea, they came there also and stirred up the crowds.

ACTS 17:10–13

People who walk the walk of faith always expect a breakthrough. ROBERT H. SCHULLER

PARTHENON ON THE ACROPOLIS, ATHENS, GREECE
Built nearly 500 years before Paul was born, the Parthenon was one of the great buildings overlooking Athens when he visited the city.

Then Paul stood in the midst of the Areopagus and said, "Men of Athens, I perceive that in all things you are very religious; for as I was passing through and considering the objects of your worship, I even found an altar with this inscription: TO THE UNKNOWN GOD. *Therefore, the One whom you worship without knowing, Him I proclaim to you: God, who made the world and everything in it, since He is Lord of heaven and earth, does not dwell in temples made with hands. Nor is He worshiped with men's hands, as though He needed anything, since He gives to all life, breath, and all things.*

ACTS 17:22–25

TEMPLE OF OLYMPIAN ZEUS, ATHENS, GREECE

The architecture, literature, and culture of Athens in Paul's day have never been surpassed. The ancient buildings that tourists admire today in Athens were dedicated to various gods in Paul's era. His strategy and wisdom were admirable when he reached out to those following the many belief systems in Athens. Instead of spending time arguing about their varying ideas, Paul drew their attention to an altar in their own city inscribed "To an unknown God." It was this God whom Paul wasted no time in proclaiming. In a city filled with monuments to other gods, he began with God, the Creator of all, and finished with God, the Judge of all. Our proclamations of Christ in today's godless cities can be confidently based, as Paul's was, on the biblical revelation of God throughout the Old and New Testaments.

If you can dream it, you can do it. ROBERT H. SCHULLER

THE AEROPAGUS OR MARS HILL, ATHENS, GREECE Paul spoke to the philosophers about Jesus in this area. Mars is the Roman name for Ares, the Greek god of war.

Great things happen when God and you confront a mountain! ROBERT H. SCHULLER

REMAINS OF THE OLD HARBOR AT CENCHREA, CORINTH, GREECE

About 500,000 people lived in Corinth when it was Greece's most important trade and commercial center. It attracted migrants, gamblers, athletes, merchants, sailors, and freed slaves. Legalized temple prostitution added to worldly amusements here. Not surprisingly, the Corinthian church, many of whose members would have come from this volatile mix of cultural, economic, social, and religious backgrounds, eventually earned Paul's most anxious letters.

He [Paul] had his hair cut off at Cenchrea, for he had taken a vow.

ACTS 18:18

Then Crispus, the ruler of the synagogue, believed on the Lord with all his household. And many of the Corinthians, hearing, believed and were baptized. Now the Lord spoke to Paul in the night by a vision, "Do not be afraid, but speak, and do not keep silent; for I am with you, and no one will attack you to hurt you; for I have many people in this city." And he continued there a year and six months, teaching the word of God among them.

ACTS 18:8–11

OLD HARBOR AT CENCHREA, CORINTH, GREECE

Cenchrea was the eastern harbor. Corinth was situated on the Isthmus of Corinth between the Ionian Sea and the Aegean Sea. Archeologists have found a marble lintel or crosspiece of a door near the residential area of Corinth. It bears the inscription "Synagogue of the Hebrews." This may well be the synagogue where Paul proclaimed the gospel in Corinth.

There is no thrill like the thrill of making a great discovery. God hides the greatest treasures in the places we least expect. ROBERT H. SCHULLER

A CAVE OVERLOOKING CORINTH, GREECE

According to tradition, it was because of the hostile response from the people of Corinth that Paul lived in this cave. He is said to have baptized people in a pool of water whose source lay here. The young shepherd pictured showed us this cave, known only to locals.

For by one Spirit we were all baptized into one body—whether Jews or Greeks, whether slaves or free—and have all been made to drink into one Spirit. For in fact the body is not one member but many. If the foot should say, "Because I am not a hand, I am not of the body," is it therefore not of the body? And if the ear should say, "Because I am not an eye, I am not of the body," is it therefore not of the body? If the whole body were an eye, where would be the hearing? If the whole were hearing, where would be the smelling? But now God has set the members, each one of them, in the body just as He pleased. And if they were all one member, where would the body be?

1 CORINTHIANS 12:13–19

And what agreement has the temple of God with idols? For you are the temple of the living God. As God has said:

"I will dwell in them and walk among them.
I will be their God, And they shall be My people."
Therefore
"Come out from among them
And be separate, says the Lord.
Do not touch what is unclean,
And I will receive you."
"I will be a Father to you,
And you shall be My sons and daughters,
Says the LORD Almighty."

Therefore, having these promises, beloved, let us cleanse ourselves from all filthiness of the flesh and spirit, perfecting holiness in the fear of God.

2 CORINTHIANS 6:16–7:1

THE TEMPLE OF APOLLO, ANCIENT CORINTH, GREECE
Apollo was the son of Zeus according to Greek and Roman mythology. This temple was built in the sixth century B.C.

God's power within me reveals the beautiful miracles about me! ROBERT H. SCHULLER

THE TOMB OF SAINT JOHN, CHURCH OF SAINT JOHN, TURKEY
Tradition holds that John's bones are buried here. The church is on the site of the Ayasuluk Fortress, a Roman necropolis about two miles from Ephesus.

And he came to Ephesus, and left them there; but he himself entered the synagogue and reasoned with the Jews. When they asked him to stay a longer time with them, he did not consent, but took leave of them, saying, "I must by all means keep this coming feast in Jerusalem; but I will return again to you, God willing." And he sailed from Ephesus.

ACTS 18:19–21

THE GREAT THEATER, EPHESUS, TURKEY
Ephesus was an important cultural center; the theater seated about 25,000 people. Tradition holds that Paul regularly preached here.

I'd rather attempt to do something big and fail, than attempt to do nothing and succeed. ROBERT H. SCHULLER

And in that day it shall be
That living waters shall flow from Jerusalem,
Half of them toward the eastern sea
And half of them toward the western sea;
In both summer and winter it shall occur.
And the LORD *shall be King over all the earth.*
In that day it shall be—
"The LORD *is one,"*
And His name one.

ZECHARIAH 14:8–9

AQUEDUCT, CAESAREA, ISRAEL
King Herod built this aqueduct in the first century B.C. It was expanded by the Romans in the second century A.D.

Jesus answered, "Most assuredly, I say to you, unless one is born of water and the Spirit, he cannot enter the kingdom of God." JOHN 3:5

No problem is too big for God's power; no person is too small for God's love. ROBERT H. SCHULLER

THE SEA FORTRESS, SIDON, LEBANON This is the Old Harbor area.

Jesus said … "Whoever desires to come after Me, let him deny himself, and take up his cross, and follow Me. For whoever desires to save his life will lose it, but whoever loses his life for My sake and the gospel's will save it. For what will it profit a man if he gains the whole world, and loses his own soul? Or what will a man give in exchange for his soul? For whoever is ashamed of Me and My words in this adulterous and sinful generation, of him the Son of Man also will be ashamed when He comes in the glory of His Father with the holy angels."

MARK 8:34–38

ROMAN AQUEDUCT AND WATERWHEEL, ORONTES RIVER, SYRIA
This was on Paul's route to Antioch. The area is well known for its waterwheels.

Jesus said … "Whoever drinks of this water will thirst again, but whoever drinks of the water that I shall give him will never thirst. But the water that I shall give him will become in him a fountain of water springing up into everlasting life."

JOHN 4:13–14

THE CARDO MAXIMUS, APAMEA, SYRIA
Paul would have walked down this very street. It was the main road to Antioch, Syria.

Love suffers long and is kind; love does not envy; love does not parade itself, is not puffed up; does not behave rudely, does not seek its own, is not provoked, thinks no evil; does not rejoice in iniquity, but rejoices in the truth; bears all things, believes all things, hopes all things, endures all things. Love never fails…

1 CORINTHIANS 13:4–8

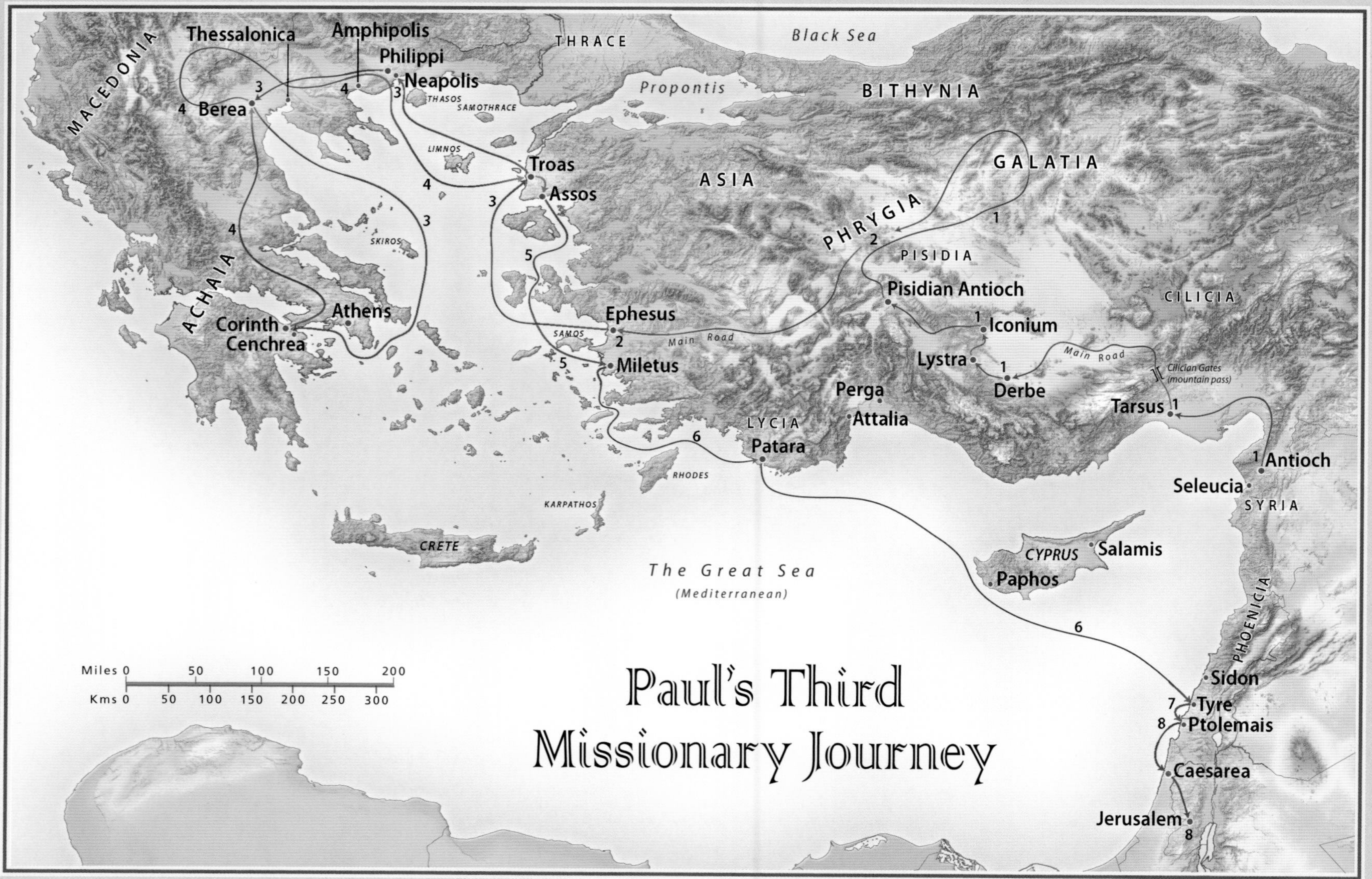

Paul's Third Missionary Journey

KEY

1. Leaving Antioch, Syria, Paul goes to Galatia via Tarsus, Derbe, Lystra, Iconium and Pisidian Antioch. Acts 18:22–23

2. From Galatia he travels through Phrygia to Ephesus. Acts 19:1, 11–20

3. He then travels through Macedonia to Corinth via Troas, Neapolis, Philippi and Berea.

4. From Corinth, Paul returns to Troas via Berea. Acts 20:3–12

5. From Troas via Assos to Miletus. Acts 20:14–15, 17–21

6. Paul leaves Miletus for Tyre, via Rhodes and Patara. Acts 21:1–6

7. Leaving Tyre, Paul travels to Ptolemais. Acts 21:7

8. Paul goes to Caesarea then on to Jerusalem. Acts 21:8–17

Lines show only general direction and approximate sequence of journeys.

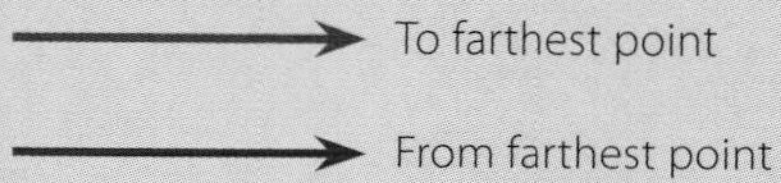

● Generally accepted or known location

MOSAIC OF PAUL PREACHING IN OLD CORINTH, GREECE

And you shall love the LORD your God with all your heart,
with all your soul, with all your mind, and with all your strength.

MARK 12:30

ACTS OF THE APOSTLES

Paul's Third Missionary Journey

Almost twenty years after Saul, the zealous persecutor of the Christian church, saw a vision and heard the voice of Jesus on the road to Damascus, Paul, the zealous proclaimer of His gospel, again saw a vision and was spoken to by the risen Christ, encouraging him to continue proclaiming the gospel.

Ready to defend himself knowledgeably from the Jewish scriptures, Paul took every opportunity to affirm God's promises to Abraham and his descendants.

When defense was not possible, Paul put aggressive opposition behind him and moved on, constantly strengthening the faith of Christ's followers. Churches that had been planted years earlier were encouraged and consolidated by Paul's fellowship, his teaching, and his servant heart.

The warmth of Paul's relationships, his humility, and his passion to carry out Christ's commission are an enduring and inspiring example to this day.

ROMAN ROAD, ANTIOCH, TURKEY
The apostles would have walked these roads.

For whatever is born of God overcomes the world. And this is the victory that has overcome the world—our faith. Who is he who overcomes the world, but he who believes that Jesus is the Son of God?

1 JOHN 5:4–5

He who dwells in the secret place of the Most High
Shall abide under the shadow of the Almighty.
I will say of the L*ORD*,
"He is my refuge and my fortress;
My God, in Him I will trust"...

He shall cover you with His feathers,
And under His wings you shall take refuge;
His truth shall be your shield and buckler.
You shall not be afraid of the terror by night,
Nor of the arrow that flies by day...

Because you have made the L*ORD*, *who is my refuge,*
Even the Most High, your dwelling place,
No evil shall befall you,
Nor shall any plague come near your dwelling;
For He shall give His angels charge over you,
To keep you in all your ways.

PSALM 91:1–11

TRADITIONAL TENT, TURKEY

The lady in the photograph made this tent using goat hair. The style and tradition of making tents in this region has not changed since Paul's time. Paul was a tent-maker and used his gift to help support himself in his mission work.

No person is too small for God's love, and no service is too insignificant for God's honor. ROBERT H. SCHULLER

DERBE, WITH THE TELL OF ANCIENT DERBE IN THE DISTANCE, TURKEY

Situated in what was once the Lycaonian region, Derbe today is located about three miles north of the city of Karaman, Turkey.

Many churches have been built in this region to commemorate Paul's visit. Paul fled to Derbe from Iconium when there was a plan to mistreat him (see Acts 14:6–20). He also visited Derbe on his second missionary journey (see Acts 16:1).

SAINT PAUL'S WELL, TARSUS, TURKEY
This is the well from which it is believed Paul would have drunk.

ROMAN AQUEDUCT, NEAR PISIDIAN ANTIOCH, TURKEY
This aqueduct would have been here at the time of Paul.

Jesus said… "If anyone thirsts, let him come to Me and drink. He who believes in Me, as the Scripture has said, out of his heart will flow rivers of living water."

JOHN 7:37–38

You can do it—become a conduit! Lord, lead me to the person you want to speak to through my life today. ROBERT H. SCHULLER

LAKE EGIRDIR, NEAR PISIDIAN ANTIOCH, TURKEY   Paul would have passed this lake on his travels.

Jesus said... "Let not your heart be troubled; you believe in God, believe also in Me." JOHN 14:1

THE LIBRARY OF CELCUS. EPHESUS. TURKEY

Ephesus was an impressive economic and cultural center in Paul's day. The record of his second journey includes an incident when sorcerers burned their scrolls, valued at 50,000 drachmas. One drachma was a day's wage for a laborer at that time.

Now God worked unusual miracles by the hands of Paul, so that even handkerchiefs or aprons were brought from his body to the sick, and the diseases left them and the evil spirits went out of them. Then some of the itinerant Jewish exorcists took it upon themselves to call the name of the Lord Jesus over those who had evil spirits, saying, "We exorcise you by the Jesus whom Paul preaches"...

And the evil spirit answered and said, "Jesus I know, and Paul I know; but who are you?"

Then the man in whom the evil spirit was leaped on them, overpowered them, and prevailed against them, so that they fled out of that house naked and wounded. This became known both to all Jews and Greeks dwelling in Ephesus; and fear fell on them all, and the name of the Lord Jesus was magnified. And many who had believed came confessing and telling their deeds. Also, many of those who had practiced magic brought their books together and burned them in the sight of all. And they counted up the value of them, and it totaled fifty thousand pieces of silver. So the word of the Lord grew mightily and prevailed.

ACTS 19:11–20

God spoke … saying: "I am the Lord *your God, who brought you out of the land of Egypt, out of the house of bondage. You shall have no other gods before Me. You shall not make for yourself a carved image—any likeness of anything that is in heaven above, or that is in the earth beneath, or that is in the water under the earth; you shall not bow down to them nor serve them …"*

EXODUS 20:1–5

THE TEMPLE OF ARTEMIS, EPHESUS

Once one of the Seven Wonders of the ancient world.

Believed to be the twin sister of Apollo, Artemis (or Diana) was one of the oldest Greek deities. Among other things, Artemis was the goddess of virginity, fertility, and childbirth. Ironically, storks now nest on one of the remaining pillars of the temple.

Never allow a fractured experience to shape your future. ROBERT H. SCHULLER

SAINT MARY'S HOUSE, EPHESUS, TURKEY

This has traditionally been known as the house where Jesus' mother Mary lived with the apostle John until her death, drinking healing waters from a fountain here. Many miracles from the water and the ash from the fireplace of this house are said to have taken place. It is highly likely that Paul visited Mary on his travels. She was the first person to accept Jesus as the Son of the Most High, even before He was born.

Mary said: " My soul magnifies the Lord,
And my spirit has rejoiced in God my Savior.
For He has regarded the lowly state of His maidservant;
For behold, henceforth all generations will call me blessed.
For He who is mighty has done great things for me,
And holy is His name.

LUKE 1:46–49

REMAINS OF THE ANCIENT HARBOR OF ALEXANDRIA, TROAS, TURKEY
Paul would have landed in this area.

OLD KAVALA (ANCIENT NEAPOLIS) AND AQUEDUCT, GREECE Paul sailed into Neapolis.

A man's life consists not of what he has, but what he is. ROBERT H. SCHULLER

STATUE SHOWING ROMAN ARMOR, FOUND IN OLD CORINTH, GREECE
This statue would have been a familiar sight when Paul was in Corinth.

To the church in Corinth, a city with much evidence of Roman power and Greek wisdom, Paul proclaimed an eternal truth—love is "a more excellent way" (1 Corinthians 13). In this city, famous for its sexual immorality, Paul's emphasis in his letters to the Corinthian church was on ethical living. To the church in Corinth, a wealthy trade center, Paul extolled the gifts of the Spirit, freely given for the good of all: "But the manifestation of the Spirit is given to each one for the profit of all" (1 Corinthians 12:7) And in this city of praiseworthy man-made monuments, Paul refers to himself as the master-builder of a church with one foundation: "For no other foundation can anyone lay than that which is laid, which is Jesus Christ" (1 Corinthians 3:11).

STONE CARVINGS OF BATTLE SCENES FROM THE THEATER, OLD CORINTH, GREECE

Therefore take up the whole armor of God, that you may be able to withstand in the evil day, and having done all, to stand. Stand therefore, having girded your waist with truth, having put on the breastplate of righteousness, and having shod your feet with the preparation of the gospel of peace; above all, taking the shield of faith with which you will be able to quench all the fiery darts of the wicked one. And take the helmet of salvation, and the sword of the Spirit, which is the word of God.

EPHESIANS 6:13–17

VIEW OVER OLD AND MODERN CORINTH, GREECE

Now thanks be to God who always leads us in triumph in Christ ... 2 CORINTHIANS 2:14

METHONI HARBOR NEAR BEREA, GREECE
Paul would have set sail for Corinth from here.

MOUNT OLYMPUS, GREECE

Paul would have seen this mountain as it was on the main thoroughfare. Mount Olympus is located in Macedonia, about sixty-two miles from Thessalonica, Greece's second largest city. Paul visited Macedonia several times and several of his fellow workers were from Macedonia. He often praised their generosity.

... we make known to you the grace of God bestowed on the churches of Macedonia: that in a great trial of affliction the abundance of their joy and their deep poverty abounded in the riches of their liberality ... beyond their ability, they were freely willing, imploring us with much urgency that we would receive the gift and the fellowship of the ministering to the saints. And not only as we had hoped, but they first gave themselves to the Lord, and then to us by the will of God.

2 CORINTHIANS 8:1–5

For every mountain there is a miracle! ROBERT H. SCHULLER

THE TEMPLE OF ATHENA, ASSOS, TURKEY
Athena was the virgin patron of Athens. The island of Lesbos is in the background. Paul would have sailed past this area.

. . . what agreement has the temple of God with idols? For you are the temple of the living God. As God has said: "I will dwell in them, and walk among them. I will be their God, and they shall be My people."

2 CORINTHIANS 6:16

And when he [Paul] met us at Assos, we took him on board and came to Mitylene. We sailed from there, and the next day came opposite Chios. The following day we arrived at Samos and stayed at Trogyllium. The next day we came to Miletus.

ACTS 20:14–15

THE THEATER, MILETUS, TURKEY

This theater was first built around 300 B.C. The Romans vastly enlarged it after 133 B.C., building three stories of seats with room for 15,000 spectators.

My decision today will become tomorrow's reality! I treat every new idea with great care. ROBERT H. SCHULLER

From Miletus he [Paul] sent to Ephesus and called for the elders of the church … he said to them: "You know, from the first day that I came to Asia, in what manner I always lived among you, serving the Lord with all humility, with many tears and trials which happened to me by the plotting of the Jews; how I kept back nothing that was helpful, but proclaimed it to you, and taught you publicly and from house to house, testifying to Jews, and also to Greeks, repentance toward God and faith toward our Lord Jesus Christ.

ACTS 20:17–21

THE SACRED WAY AND IONIC STOA AT MILETUS, TURKEY

You can often measure a person by the size of their dream. ROBERT H. SCHULLER

OLD HARBOR ENTRY TO RHODES, GREECE
This harbor entry dates from before Paul's time.

Now it came to pass, that when we had departed from them and set sail, running a straight course we came to Cos, the following day to Rhodes, and from there to Patara. And finding a ship sailing over to Phoenicia, we went aboard and set sail.

ACTS 21:1–2

LINDOS, RHODES, GREECE
Paul would have visited this area.

Keep your heart right, and your faith will burn bright. ROBERT H. SCHULLER

SAINT PAUL'S HARBOR FROM THE ACROPOLIS, LINDOS, RHODES, GREECE The safe harbor where Paul stayed while in this area is shown on the left.

For you will be His witness to all men of what you have seen and heard. ACTS 22:15

ARCH OF MODESTUS, PATARA, TURKEY

Jesus said … "Behold, I stand at the door and knock. If anyone hears My voice and opens the door, I will come in to him and dine with him, and he with Me. To him who overcomes I will grant to sit with Me on My throne, as I also overcame and sat down with My Father on His throne. He who has an ear, let him hear what the Spirit says to the churches.

REVELATION 3:20–22

Let us hold fast the confession of our hope without wavering, for He who promised is faithful. And let us consider one another in order to stir up love and good works, not forsaking the assembling of ourselves together, as is the manner of some, but exhorting one another, and so much the more as you see the Day approaching.

HEBREWS 10:23–25

TOMBS OF THE KINGS, PAPHOS, CYPRUS, GREECE

On his way back to Jerusalem, Paul may have stopped here to visit and encourage the churches in this area. When Christianity was unpopular, Christians continued to find ways to meet together in worship. These tombs provided a gathering place in times of danger.

BOAT HARBOR, TYRE, LEBANON

There was a real strength and bond between the early Christians as their beliefs had been tested by a lot of hardship and persecution. Although Paul was in a hurry to get back to Jerusalem, he spent a week with the Christian community in this area. Paul may or may not have known the followers at Tyre, but they fellowshipped with him gladly as they were one in Christ.

When we had sighted Cyprus, we passed it on the left, sailed to Syria, and landed at Tyre; for there the ship was to unload her cargo. And finding disciples, we stayed there seven days. They told Paul through the Spirit not to go up to Jerusalem.

ACTS 21:3–4

Be thankful for the storms of your life that have blown out, blown over, or passed you by and never touched you. ROBERT H. SCHULLER

BOAT HARBOR AND SEA WALL, ACRE (ANCIENT PTOLEMAIS), ISRAEL

. . . from Tyre, we came to Ptolemais, greeted the brethren, and stayed with them one day. ACTS 21:7

... we who were Paul's companions ... came to Caesarea, and entered the house of Philip the evangelist, who was one of the seven, and stayed with him. Now this man had four virgin daughters who prophesied. And as we stayed many days, a certain prophet named Agabus came down from Judea. When he had come to us, he took Paul's belt, bound his own hands and feet, and said, "Thus says the Holy Spirit, 'So shall the Jews at Jerusalem bind the man who owns this belt, and deliver him into the hands of the Gentiles.' " Now when we heard these things, both we and those from that place pleaded with him not to go up to Jerusalem. Then Paul answered, "What do you mean by weeping and breaking my heart? For I am ready not only to be bound, but also to die at Jerusalem for the name of the Lord Jesus." So when he would not be persuaded, we ceased, saying, "The will of the Lord be done."

ACTS 21:8–14

MAIN BEACH, CAESAREA, ISRAEL

Do not be overcome by evil, but overcome evil with good. ROMANS 12:21

As you walk the walk of faith you live without insurance, but your faith is your assurance. ROBERT H. SCHULLER

KEY

1. Paul leaves Jerusalem for Caesarea after addressing a mob. Acts 21:40–23:35

2. In Caesarea he is taken before Felix the governor and his successor Festus. Acts 24–26:32

3. Paul travels from Caesarea to Sidon via Tyre, then to Myra. Acts 27:1–6

4. He sails on to Fair Havens, Crete via Cnidus. Acts 27:7–12

5. Battling a storm his ship sails on to Malta. Acts 27:13–44. Paul heals Publius' father on Malta. Acts 28:7–8

6. From Malta Paul sails to Syracuse, Sicily. Acts 28:11–12

7. Paul arrives at Reggio Calabria (Rhegium), Italy. Acts 28:13

8. Paul sails on via Vietri Sul Mare in the area of Pompeii.

9. At Puteoli, Paul is met by friends. Acts 28:13–14

10. Paul leaves Puteoli for Rome. Friends meet him at the Forum of Appius. Acts 28:15

11. Via Appia Antica (the old Appian Way) and the Pontine Marshes, Paul arrives in Rome. Acts 28:16

Lines show only general direction and approximate sequence of journeys.

→ Paul's Journey to Rome

● Generally accepted or known location

PAINTING, SAINT ANANIAS' CHURCH, DAMASCUS, SYRIA

Finally, my brethren, be strong in the Lord and in the power of His might.

EPHESIANS 6:10

ACTS OF THE APOSTLES

Paul's Journey to Rome

Despite being warned by the prophet Agabus that he would be arrested in Jerusalem, Paul did not change the destination of his third journey; the prophet had not suggested he shouldn't go on. Paul was staying in Caesarea with Philip, who had lived there for more than twenty years. His four daughters were prophetesses, but they had not been led by the Spirit to warn Paul not to go. Paul's submission to the will of God was total. His trust in the leading of the Holy Spirit compelled him to go on to Jerusalem. He was prepared to die for his Master.

A few days after his arrival there, Paul was arrested, but he was still in control. In handcuffs, he exercised complete freedom in Christ. In the midst of the threat to his life in Jerusalem, he was dignified and unafraid. During the subsequent sea voyage to Rome, during the violent storm, the shipwreck, and the snake-bite on Malta, he was calm and cooperative. During his trials before Jewish and Roman leaders, Paul demonstrated extraordinary confidence, courage, and faith.

The whole process of his arrest and his dramatic journey to Rome was not without positives. He used the opportunity presented by his arrest to tell his full testimony to a large crowd in Jerusalem, beginning with the stoning of Stephen many years earlier. He passionately challenged the legality of the high priest; he boldly spoke to Governor Felix about faith in Jesus Christ; he cured many who were ill in Malta; and he encouraged believers along the way. In Rome itself, still under house arrest, and without oppression from the imperial government, he gave two years of outstanding service to the Lord who had first called him on the road to Damascus.

Paul's life clearly demonstrates the transforming power of the Holy Spirit expressed through a man who was willing to serve Jesus with all that he had.

Total peace will only come from total commitment. ROBERT H. SCHULLER

WESTERN ENTRANCE TO THE TEMPLE MOUNT, JERUSALEM, ISRAEL
Not long after Paul's arrival in Jerusalem, he was seen in the temple by Jews from Asia who stirred up the crowd against him. They accused him of teaching and acting contrary to Jewish law. The mob turned violent and tried to kill Paul, but the commander of the Roman garrison intervened and arrested him. When the commander could not ascertain the truth because of the uproar, he ordered that Paul be taken into the barracks. Paul had to be carried by the soldiers because of the violence of the mob.

ANTONIA FORTRESS, JERUSALEM, ISRAEL

Less than thirty years after Jesus took up His cross here, Paul was held in protective custody in the barracks before beginning his final journey to Rome. Stairs connected the fortress with the temple area.

[While Paul was being held in the barracks] The Lord stood by him and said, "Be of good cheer, Paul; for as you have testified for Me in Jerusalem, so you must also bear witness at Rome."

ACTS 23:11

Jesus said … "O Jerusalem, Jerusalem, the one who kills the prophets and stones those who are sent to her! How often I wanted to gather your children together, as a hen gathers her brood under her wings, but you were not willing!

LUKE 13:34

The cross is not a negative, but a positive symbol. It is a giant minus turned into the biggest plus sign in the history of the human race. ROBERT H. SCHULLER

SUNSET OVER JERUSALEM, ISRAEL

Paul left Jerusalem with a clear conscience. He had proclaimed Christ to the people of Jerusalem. When some men formed a conspiracy to kill him, the Roman commander sent him to Caesarea with a letter for Felix, the governor: "This man was seized by the Jews and was about to be killed by them. Coming with the troops I rescued him, having learned that he was a Roman [citizen]. And when I wanted to know the reason they accused him, I brought him before their council. I found out that he was accused concerning questions of their law, but had nothing charged against him deserving of death or chains. And when it was told me that the Jews lay in wait for the man, I sent him immediately to you, and also commanded his accusers to state before you the charges against him" (Acts 23:27–30)

The commander judged the danger so great that he sent Paul to Caesarea guarded by two centurions, two hundred soldiers, seventy horsemen, and two hundred spearmen. Here was a man whose bold faith in Jesus provoked incredible passion among his enemies. Are we prepared to face the consequences of an uncompromising stand for Him?

HIPPODROME, CAESAREA, ISRAEL

Built by Herod the Great, the arena of the Hippodrome once held 20,000 spectators at chariot races. Paul would have seen this place and may have even visited it.

Because of his witness, Paul suffered many imprisonments. One was at Caesarea, the great coastal city of Palestine. Here Paul spent two years in prison and appeared before two governors who tried his case: Festus and Felix.

Festus decided Paul was to be granted freedom; but Paul declined his own release in favor of a greater goal. He wished to stay in prison in order to have the chance to speak to Caesar. As a Roman citizen, Paul had the right to appeal his case to the emperor. Festus told Paul he would be free had it not been for his request. Paul had appealed to Caesar, so to Caesar he would go.

Paul was willing to attempt to do great things for God even if it meant further imprisonment. But the cost was worth the opportunity to speak to one of the world's great leaders about the greatest event in history. The book of Philippians reveals the outcome of Paul's plan. "All the saints greet you, but especially those who are of Caesar's household" (4:22) Paul's message of Jesus Christ infiltrated the mighty kingdom of Caesar.

What goal would you set for yourself if you knew you would not fail? Who is the Caesar—the greater authority, the powerful overlord—in your life? Appeal to Caesar; speak of Christ confidently no matter what the personal cost. DR. ROBERT H. SCHULLER

Paul said … "being confident of this very thing, that He who has begun a good work in you will complete it until the day of Jesus Christ." PHILIPPIANS 1:6

ROCK-CUT TOMBS, MYRA, TURKEY
On Paul's journey to Rome, the centurion escorting him changed ships at Myra. The Roman Empire had a fleet of vessels taking grain from Egypt to Italy, so it was possible that Paul sailed on a grain ship.

ANDRIKAE PORT, MYRA, TURKEY

This is the old entry to Myra Port, near the river mouth leading to Myra. A thick chain was stretched across the mouth of the river during Paul's era to prevent enemies from reaching the city.

And when we had sailed over the sea which is off Cilicia and Pamphylia, we came to Myra, a city of Lycia. There the centurion found an Alexandrian ship sailing to Italy, and he put us on board.

ACTS 27:5–6

Prayer brings me peace in the midst of a storm. ROBERT H. SCHULLER

SAINT PAUL'S CHURCH, CRETE, GREECE

The bay described in Acts as 'Fair Havens' is now called Kalio Limenes. It is still a sleepy village. The church was built close to a cave where it is believed Paul took shelter.

ICON OF SAINT PAUL, KALIO LIMENES, CRETE, GREECE

When we had sailed slowly many days, and arrived with difficulty off Cnidus, the wind not permitting us to proceed, we sailed under the shelter of Crete off Salmone. Passing it with difficulty, we came to a place called Fair Havens, near the city of Lasea. ACTS 27:7–8

Your life can be the portrait of a survivor. ROBERT H. SCHULLER

PAINTING OF PAUL PREACHING AT KALIO LIMENES (FAIR HAVENS), CRETE, GREECE

PAINTING OF PAUL LEAVING TITUS ON CRETE, GREECE

Now when much time had been spent, and sailing was now dangerous because the Fast was already over, Paul advised them, saying, "Men, I perceive that this voyage will end with disaster and much loss, not only of the cargo and ship, but also our lives." Nevertheless the centurion was more persuaded by the helmsman and the owner of the ship than by the things spoken by Paul. And because the harbor was not suitable to winter in, the majority advised to set sail from there also, if by any means they could reach Phoenix, a harbor of Crete opening toward the southwest and northwest, and winter there.

ACTS 27:9–12

Titus was an uncircumcised Gentile. Paul introduced him to the church elders in Jerusalem as an example that Gentiles do not need to be circumcised in order to receive God's salvation. Because of false teaching and immorality on Crete, Paul left Titus there to teach and instruct the churches. Church tradition holds that Titus was the first bishop of Crete.

THE HOLY CHURCH OF TITUS, CRETE, GREECE
It is claimed that the skull of Titus, who died around A.D. 100, is located here.

This is a faithful saying … that those who have believed in God should be careful to maintain good works.

TITUS 3:8

To Titus, a true son in our common faith: Grace, mercy, and peace from God the Father and the Lord Jesus Christ our Savior. For this reason I left you in Crete, that you should set in order the things that are lacking, and appoint elders in every city as I commanded you.

TITUS 1:4–5

Faith! Don't live life—or leave life—without it! ROBERT H. SCHULLER

They sailed close by Crete. But not long after, a tempestuous head wind arose, called Euroclydon. So when the ship was caught, and could not head into the wind, we let her drive. And running under the shelter of an island called Clauda, we secured the skiff with difficulty. When they had taken it on board, they used cables to undergird the ship; and fearing lest they should run aground on the Syrtis Sands, they struck sail and so were driven. And because we were exceedingly tempest-tossed, the next day they lightened the ship.

Now when neither sun nor stars appeared for many days, and no small tempest beat on us, all hope that we would be saved was finally given up. But after long abstinence from food, then Paul stood in the midst of them and said, "Men, you should have listened to me, and not have sailed from Crete and incurred this disaster and loss. And now I urge you to take heart, for there will be no loss of life among you, but only of the ship. For there stood by me this night an angel of the God to whom I belong and whom I serve, saying, 'Do not be afraid, Paul; you must be brought before Caesar; and indeed God has granted you all those who sail with you.' Therefore take heart, men, for I believe God that it will be just as it was told me. However, we must run aground on a certain island."

Now when the fourteenth night had come, as we were driven up and down in the Adriatic Sea, about midnight the sailors took soundings. They dropped four anchors from the stern, and prayed for day to come. And as the sailors were seeking to escape from the ship Paul said to the centurion and the soldiers, "Unless these men stay in the ship, you cannot be saved." Paul implored them all to take food, saying, "Today is the fourteenth day you have eaten nothing. Take nourishment since not a hair will fall from the head of any of you." He took bread and gave thanks to God in the presence of them all; and when he had broken it he began to eat. Then they also took food themselves. And in all we were two hundred and seventy-six persons on the ship. So when they had eaten enough they threw out the wheat into the sea.

When it was day they ran the ship aground; and the stern was being broken up by the violence of the waves. And the soldiers' plan was to kill the prisoners. But the centurion, wanting to save Paul, commanded that those who could swim should jump overboard first and get to land, and the rest, some on boards and some on parts of the ship. And so it was that they all escaped safely to land.

(See ACTS 27:13–44)

FRESCO, THE CHURCH OF SAINT PAUL'S SHIPWRECK, VALETTA, MALTA

Paul's shipwreck was an accident, but it resulted in the establishment of the Christian church in Malta. God can bring great good out of the worst situation!

ICON, CHURCH OF SAINT PAUL'S SHIPWRECK, VALETTA, MALTA

This iconic statue is reputed to hold a piece of bone from Paul's arm. While Paul was shipwrecked here, he healed the father of Publius, the chief official of the island.

And it happened that the father of Publius lay sick of a fever and dysentery. Paul went in to him and prayed, and he laid his hands on him and healed him. So when this was done, the rest of those on the island who had diseases also came and were healed. They also honored us in many ways; and when we departed, they provided such things as were necessary.

ACTS 28:8–10

ICON, CHURCH OF SAINT PAUL'S SHIPWRECK, VALETTA, MALTA

This is said to be part of the pillar on which Paul was beheaded. This piece matches the other part of the pillar, which is in Italy (shown on page 194).

ICON, SAINT PAUL'S CHURCH, RABAT, MALTA

This iconic statue is also reputed to hold a piece of bone from Paul's arm.

He who does not love does not know God, for God is love. 1 JOHN 4:8

SUNRISE, GRAND HARBOR, VALETTA, MALTA

For you are all sons of God through faith in Christ Jesus. GALATIANS 3:26

SAINT PAUL'S BAY, MALTA

The island to the left is where the shipwreck of Paul took place.

SAINT PAUL'S GROTTO, SAINT PAUL'S CHURCH, RABAT, MALTA

This is the place where Paul was incarcerated while in Malta.

Attempt great things for God—expect great things from God. ROBERT H. SCHULLER

SYRACUSE HARBOR, SICILY, ITALY
Paul came here from Malta and stayed three days.

After three months we sailed in an Alexandrian ship whose figurehead was the Twin Brothers, which had wintered at the island. And landing at Syracuse, we stayed three days.

ACTS 28:11–12

CRYPT OF SAINT MARCIAN, SAN GIOVANNI EVANGELISTA CHURCH, SYRACUSE, SICILY, ITALY

It is believed that Marcian was instructed by the apostle Peter and that he is buried in these catacombs. These are the most extensive paleo-Christian catacombs found outside Rome. Saint Giovanni's Evangelista Church is built above them. It is believed Paul preached here to the local Christian community and Saint Paul's Altar is said to be the exact spot from which he spoke. It is characteristic of Paul's incisive messages that he preached in a place of death about Jesus Christ, the giver of new life.

SAINT PAUL'S ALTAR IN THE CRYPT

Jesus said … "I am the way, the truth, and the life. No one comes to the Father except through Me.

JOHN 14:6

The most important thing is living your life for something more important than your life! ROBERT H. SCHULLER

SCILLA, NEAR REGGIO CALABRIA, ITALY

Paul would have sailed past this place on his way to Rome. His journey to Rome was the climax of all that he had endured in the service of his Savior. In a letter to the Corinthian believers he wrote about some of the things that he had overcome.

... in labors more abundant, in stripes above measure, in prisons more frequently, in deaths often ... five times I received forty stripes minus one. Three times I was beaten with rods; once I was stoned [left for dead]; three times I was shipwrecked; a night and a day I have been in the deep; in journeys often, in perils of waters, in perils of robbers, in perils of my own countrymen, in perils of the Gentiles, in perils in the city, in perils in the wilderness, in perils in the sea, in perils among false brethren; in weariness and toil, in sleeplessness often, in hunger and thirst, in fastings often, in cold and nakedness—besides the other things, what comes upon me daily: my deep concern for all the churches.

2 CORINTHIANS 11:23–28

THE BURNT COLUMN OF SAINT PAUL, REGGIO CALABRIA, ITALY

It is believed that when Paul came to the city then known as Rhegium, he preached by candlelight. The candle kept burning miraculously. The column is said to have burn marks from that candle.

... we circled round and reached Rhegium. And after one day the south wind blew; and the next day we came to Puteoli ...

ACTS 28:13

THE CATHEDRAL OF REGGIO CALABRIA, HOME OF THE BURNT COLUMN

Your cross will turn into your crown. ROBERT H. SCHULLER

VIETRI SUL MARE (SOUTH OF NAPLES), ITALY Paul would have sailed past this area.

But the fruit of the Spirit is love, joy, peace, longsuffering, kindness, goodness, faithfulness … GALATIANS 5:22

THE VILLA DEI MISTERI, POMPEII, ITALY
This fresco from the home of a noble shows the lifestyle during the time when Paul may have visited Pompeii.

UNDER THE FLAVIO AMPHITHEATER, PUTEOLI, ITALY (LEFT AND RIGHT)
Paul was invited by believers living in Puteoli to stay for a week. He may well have visited this amphitheater which in later years became a place where Christians were persecuted for their faith.

... the next day we came to Puteoli, where we found brethren, and were invited to stay with them seven days. And so we went toward Rome.

ACTS 28:13–14

VIEW OF SEZZE FROM THE FORUM APPII, ITALY Located forty-three miles southeast of Rome at the beginning of the Pontine Marshes, Forum Appii was where Christians from Rome came to greet Paul.

Love does no harm to a neighbor; therefore love is the fulfillment of the law. ROMANS 13:10

To all who are in Rome, beloved of God, called to be saints: Grace to you and peace from God our Father and the Lord Jesus Christ. First, I thank my God through Jesus Christ for you all, that your faith is spoken of throughout the whole world. For God is my witness, whom I serve with my spirit in the gospel of His Son, that without ceasing I make mention of you always in my prayers, making request if, by some means, now at last I may find a way in the will of God to come to you. For I long to see you, that I may impart to you some spiritual gift …

ROMANS 1:7–11

FIELD OF SUNFLOWERS, THE PONTINE MARSHES, ITALY

The marshes have now been drained and reclaimed. Three years before his journey to Rome, Paul had promised the Roman Christians that he would visit them. Now, as a prisoner, he would finally meet some of them face-to-face in this place. Their long journey on foot, some forty-three miles from Rome, would surely have warmed the loving heart of the apostle.

Faith is the natural blossom of someone who loves. ROBERT H. SCHULLER

AQUEDUCT ON THE VIA APPIA ANTICA (OLD APPIAN WAY), ITALY

Paul would have passed this on the final leg of his journey to Rome.

THE VIA APPIA ANTICA (OLD APPIAN WAY), ITALY

... so we went toward Rome. And from there, when the brethren heard about us, they came to meet us as far as Appii Forum and Three Inns. When Paul saw them, he thanked God and took courage.

ACTS 28:14–15

THE FORUM, ROME, ITALY Paul was probably judged in this area by the Roman government before being imprisoned.

... all things work together for good to those who love God, to those who are the called according to His purpose. ROMANS 8:28

Let go and let God take over. ROBERT H. SCHULLER

THE STADIUM OF DOMITIAN AT PALATINE HILL, ROME, ITALY
Paul would have seen this area.

As a Jew of the highest order (Acts 26:4–5) Paul's love for the Jewish nation was such that his last recorded dialogue in the book of Acts was an appeal to the Jews to believe that by His Spirit, God was calling His ancient people to believe in Jesus as the One the scriptures had foretold—the One He had spoken about through Isaiah, one of the greatest Jewish prophets.

"The Holy Spirit spoke rightly through Isaiah the prophet to our fathers, saying,
'Go to this people and say:
"Hearing you will hear, and shall not understand;
And seeing you will see, and not perceive;
For the hearts of this people have grown dull.
Their ears are hard of hearing,
And their eyes they have closed,
Lest they should see with their eyes and hear with their ears,
Lest they should understand with their hearts and turn,
So that I should heal them."' "

ACTS 28:25–27

THE MAMERTINE PRISON, ROME, ITALY

According to tradition, both Peter and Paul were imprisoned here. It is believed that they drank water from this well, and were chained to the pillar by the altar. Prisoners and guards are thought to have been baptized with water from this well.

THE BASILICA OF SAINT PAUL OUTSIDE THE WALLS, ROME, ITALY

This is the second largest basilica in Rome, and Paul's remains are said to be buried in a sarcophagus underneath it. Its full name indicates its location beyond the ancient walls surrounding the center of Rome.

THE CHURCH OF SAINT PAUL, THREE FOUNTAINS, OUTSIDE ROME, ITALY
The painting depicts the beheading of Paul.

THE CHURCH OF SAINT PAUL, THREE FOUNTAINS, ITALY
The pillar on which it is said Paul was beheaded.

INTERIOR OF THE CHURCH OF SAINT PAUL,
THREE FOUNTAINS, ITALY

Located near Rome this church was raised over the location where it is believed Paul was beheaded on Nero's orders. Legend says that when his head was severed from the body, it bounced three times, and wherever it struck the earth a fountain sprang up. These springs are still flowing, and the fountains are in the sanctuary itself.

Love is … deciding to make your problem my problem. ROBERT H. SCHULLER

ALTAR INSIDE THE BASILICA OF SAINT JOHN LATERAN, ROME, ITALY

The beautiful *baldacchino* over the High Altar, which looks out of place in its present surroundings, dates back to 1369. At the top is a reliquary said to contain the heads of Peter and Paul.

Paul was so passionate about Jesus he was always talking about Him. Paul had been forgiven much in his life, and often those who have been forgiven much love much. We speak about the things we love, so how much do we talk about Jesus?

Paul said … "For I am already being poured out as a drink offering, and the time of my departure is at hand. I have fought the good fight, I have finished the race, I have kept the faith. Finally, there is laid up for me the crown of righteousness, which the Lord, the righteous Judge, will give to me on that Day, and not to me only but also to all who have loved His appearing."

2 TIMOTHY 4:6–8

THE BASILICA OF SAINT JOHN LATERAN ON THE CELIAN HILL, ROME, ITALY

Peter said … "Repent, and let every one of you be baptized in the name of Jesus Christ for the remission of sins; and you shall receive the gift of the Holy Spirit. For the promise is to you and to your children, and to all who are afar off …"

ACTS 2:38–39

Peter said… "Since you have purified your souls in obeying the truth through the Spirit in sincere love of the brethren, love one another fervently with a pure heart, having been born again, not of corruptible seed but incorruptible, through the word of God which lives and abides forever, because

'All flesh is as grass,
And all the glory of man as the flower of the grass.
The grass withers,
And its flower falls away,
But the word of the LORD endures forever.'

Now this is the word which by the gospel was preached to you."

1 PETER 1:22–25

The Lord is my shepherd;
I shall not want.
He makes me to lie down in green pastures;
He leads me beside the still waters.
He restores my soul;
He leads me in the paths of righteousness
For His name's sake.
Yea, though I walk through the valley of the shadow of death,
I will fear no evil;
For You are with me;
Your rod and Your staff, they comfort me.
You prepare a table before me in the presence of my enemies;
You anoint my head with oil;
My cup runs over.
Surely goodness and mercy shall follow me
All the days of my life;
And I will dwell in the house of the Lord
Forever.

PSALM 23:1–6

SUNRISE OVER THE SEA OF GALILEE FROM MOUNT ARBEL, ISRAEL

The voice of the Lord is over the waters. PSALM 29:3

MOSAIC DETAIL, INTERIOR OF BASILICA OF THE TRANSFIGURATION, MT TABOR, ISRAEL.

The death and resurrection of Jesus heralded a new age—the age of the Spirit.

The law had told people what to do, but it did not offer the will or the power to obey moral and just principles. The gift of the Holy Spirit, the same Spirit who dwelt with Christ as He accomplished His work on earth, provides us with both the will and the power to live Christ's way daily.

The apostles were clearly empowered by His Spirit, and countless men and women in this age of the Spirit have also brought glory to God in His power, and in submission to His loving will.

The grace of the Lord Jesus Christ, and the love of God,
and the communion of the Holy Spirit be with you all. Amen.

2 CORINTHIANS 13:14

The LORD bless you and keep you;
The LORD make His face shine upon you,
And be gracious to you;
The LORD lift up His countenance upon you,
And give you peace.

NUMBERS 6:24–26